Getting Onside -
A Practical Guide to Low-Cost Football Marketing

Ian Fitzpatrick
Getting Onside – A Practical Guide to Low-Cost Football
Marketing

About The Author

Ian Fitzpatrick is the Chief Marketing Officer for Stenhousemuir Football Club, currently playing in League Two in Scotland. He is also Senior Marketing Strategy Manager at Buzz Bingo, the UK's largest omni-channel bingo operator.

He has gained qualifications in Marketing, including a Diploma in Digital Marketing, from CIM [Chartered Institute of Marketing] and in Social Media Marketing from IDM [Institute of Data and Marketing].

He has provided marketing support to a variety of football clubs in Scotland and has held official roles in several senior football clubs.

In the summer of 2023 Ian launched the online Scottish Football Media Discord group which allows media team members from all levels of football to help and support each other, with the overall goal of making Scottish Football a more attractive proposition for fans and sponsors.

Table of Contents

Introduction

This book is designed to help to build content for, and market, a football club, and has been written with a business outlook in mind. It is predominantly aimed at clubs at the lower end of the pyramid with little or no marketing budgets. Given the low costs of social media marketing, this book heavily leans on using social media as your main marketing tool.

Although your main content will be around the matchday experience, you should also use your marketing to promote your club as a business and this book will help you manage your social media accounts as such.

The book is split into three sections;

1. **Short Term – The basics**
   o These are the basics that you should cover at any level. They involve limited output while still giving your club content a professional feel

2. **Medium Term – Taking your content to the next level**
   o These are activities that you should look to undertake once you've mastered the basics. These will help you take your marketing to the next level

3. **Long Term – Mastering football marketing**
   o These are the actions of a skilled marketer. By following this book, you will be able to execute these longer-term goals - regardless of your existing knowledge or skill set

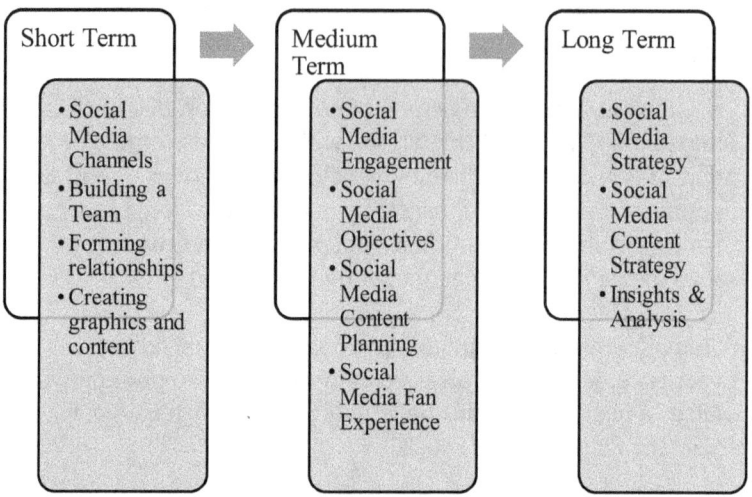

Short Term
- Social Media Channels
- Building a Team
- Forming relationships
- Creating graphics and content

Medium Term
- Social Media Engagement
- Social Media Objectives
- Social Media Content Planning
- Social Media Fan Experience

Long Term
- Social Media Strategy
- Social Media Content Strategy
- Insights & Analysis

Documents mentioned throughout this book are available for free at our dedicated web page. https://bit.ly/FootballMarketing

Why did I write this book?

This book is the culmination of several years of work. During the COVID lockdowns, I reached out to help and support local football clubs with their marketing and social media strategies.

I realised that there was little support in the sense of marketing a lower league football club and decided to build a document that I could share with these clubs to help with their social media marketing and engagement.

As we moved away from COVID, I took a role at Stenhousemuir FC who currently play in the fourth level of Scottish football. Again, looking around for any helpful books was not getting me very far. So, using the knowledge I have built up over the years, I decided to pull together a book that will help people that were in my situation.

This book has been written to give anyone working at a football club a basic, intermediate and expert approach to running their club's marketing department either on their own, or as part of a team.

Who am I talking to?

This book is targeted at anyone who is currently working at, or wants to work at, a football club's marketing department.

The book is split into three parts and some people may not find all three parts useful. Some may just opt for a basic understanding and help while some may find the full book beneficial. If you're looking to create a career of any form in marketing, then there's a lot of information in this book that will help you on your journey.

Short Term - The Basics

Team Building & Essential Roles

This section is used to help you build a team as well and define the key roles that you'll need to fill. My recommended head count may differ from what you have available at your club, but the roles and tasks undertaken should be standard.

The Perfect Team

Given that you'll most likely rely on a team of volunteers, it may be difficult to build the perfect team.

The perfect team should have the mixture of experience and skills to help you cover the three key areas of football marketing:

- Graphic Design
- Photography
- Videography

While there are three main roles, you may not need three different people as a single person can cover more than one task. For example, a photographer could also be a skilled graphic designer.

The perfect team would consist of:

- **Head of Media**
  - This person will manage the team, create strategy and objectives, plan content, and analyse results. They may also take up other roles within the team, such as videographer, photographer or graphic designer.

- **Media Officer**
    - This person will usually oversee scheduling and posting content. This role is not essential but allows the Head of Media to focus on the bigger picture planning and strategy elements. Without this role, the Head of Media would need to schedule and post the content.

- **Graphic Designer**
    - **Creating good graphics** is a key role in your club, but this does not mean that you need to have a highly skilled graphic designer. There is enough software out there to build basic graphics for use throughout the season. Software like *Canva* [https://www.canva.com] can help make basic graphics, whereas more skilled software [such as Photoshop] will need an element of expertise. If the budget is available, you can purchase a suit of bespoke graphics templates from a paid designer that you can use and amend as the season goes on.

- **Photographer**
    - Another key role for your club is a photographer. Although beneficial, there's no need to have a photographer on hand for every game. The minimum you should look for in a photographer is to cover a media shoot, one home match and one away match. This should give you enough content to build your matchday graphics, as well as creating a set of action shots with both home and away kits. Again, if you can't find a volunteer for this role, you should consider the benefits of paying a professional to provide for the minimum as above.

        If you do pay for help, you must clarify with the photographer that you will have the rights to use the images across all of your website, social and print requirements.

- **Videographer**
  - Depending on your level, this should be a crucial, and probably most difficult to fill, role. A videographer will be responsible for recording matches and building the matchday highlights package. This can be a role that needs little skills to execute, but it is a disciplined role and could require the equipment to be purchased by the club to support the role.

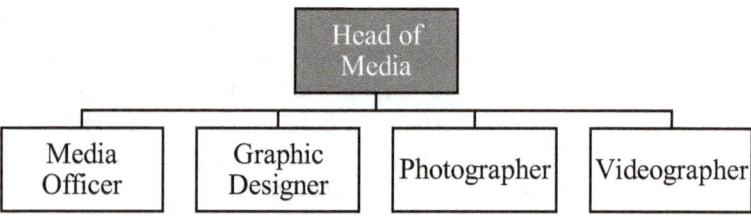

This would be the perfect team for clubs at most levels and will help you to cover all bases. You may get lucky and have several people in each role which will help ensure that there's always cover available.

I am sure that many people reading this will be looking at that chart and wondering about how they can do this all on their own. You should never be scared to ask for help. Use your social media channels looking for club volunteers. You can join the Scottish Football Media Discord group to help you find volunteers. https://discord.gg/FdFFEeKM

Although you're more than likely not going to be able to recruit for paid roles, you should always look to compensate volunteers where possible. As a minimum, this could be by covering travelling expenses, but look out for other ways to say 'thank you' for their time, for instance, by supplying some club leisurewear.

9

When building your team, be sure to look locally at schools, colleges or universities with classes that could be beneficial. If you have a local student population, there could be mutual benefits for the two parties.

Building Internal & External Relationships

This section is used to help you build relationships both internally and externally. By building internal relationships, you can create supporters within the club that will help you deliver your marketing goals. By building external relationships, you can easily build yourself a useful support network across other clubs, local newspapers, photographers etc. This will help you generate content, build ideas and provide support at hand if you need it.

Internal Relationship Building

Whenever you start at a club, you should quickly make yourself known to everyone at all levels.

Ensure that the Chairman and Board know who you are and what your goals are for the club and your role. These are the people who will support you as you build on your plans to help the club. If you need investment in equipment, it's this group that will choose whether to supply you with what you need. Please don't jump into a board meeting with a list of demands on your first day, as you'll most likely receive a knock-back and make a bad first impression. Start small and start sharing the plans which you think will help you going forward. If there's important equipment that you need quickly, ensure that you pull together the relevant information to show why it's important and how it will help you achieve your, and your clubs, goals. If you are able to, you may have more success if you can demonstrate real returns on the board's investment. The more you build this relationship, the more likely the board will be happy to support your requests.

Ensure that any back-office staff know who you are as they are key to helping you succeed. Make sure that you're kept up to date with player signings, player releases, birthdays etc. By having this knowledge in a timely manner, you can plan your content accordingly. Where possible, it's also beneficial to share some focus on the staff. For instance, where you may not have a match week, you can highlight some of the staff or volunteers who work behind the scenes, putting them into focus and allowing the fanbase to see how much work goes in behind the scenes.

Build a strong relationship with the manager and players. Make sure that you find out what the manager is looking for when it comes to social media content, and where their boundaries lie. Some managers may be happy to let you record training sessions or adding a camera to the dugout during match days, others may not. Make sure that you're aware of what the manager is and isn't comfortable with.

Make sure you get to know the players and that they know who you are. It will help massively when you're looking at pre- or post-match content. It's also important that you spread your content focus across the whole squad. Helping to bring the fans and players closer together is a major part of your role, and you should look to do this with all players, and not just the fan favourites.

External Relationship Building

As well as building relationships inside the club, it's just as important to build external relationships.

Make sure to introduce yourself to local reporters and photographers. This may be as simple as looking for contact on social media. There may also be a list already prepared at the club, so ask around to see if this exists. Reporters can help promote your club in local newspapers and photographers can help you cover some of your basic requirements, though this will most likely come at a cost.

You should look to build up relationships with local businesses, especially if they already have a relationship with the club.

For example, if you have a main sponsor at the club who owns a restaurant or local shop, you should look for opportunities to have kit launches or player signings at these locations. This strengthens the relationship and may help future sponsorship decisions to benefit the club.

It's also beneficial to get to know lecturers at any local schools, colleges or universities that cover media, or marketing classes. By having these relationships in place, you're opening opportunities to be able to talk to students who may be interested in building a portfolio of work with your club.

Finally, there is one more relationship that is very often overlooked. It's vital to build relationships with media teams at other clubs either locally, or in the same league. By building these relationships, you can share ideas, suggestions or even resources. If you're struggling to find a videographer to cover a match, having a good relationship with a member of the other team, you could even ask to share footage. Whether or not they do will be a club decision, but by having a pre-existing strong relationship with the club, or even better, media team, you will strengthen your position should you need help. Equally, by helping other clubs, so long as it's not at the detriment to your club, you can help build these relationships and curate yourself a good reputation within the community.

Creating Graphics & Other Content

This section helps you identify what graphics and content you should create to help your club and how to go about making and generating content. The graphics you use for each matchday should tell your matchday story. Your build up will consist of your pre-match content such as previews, key match information and infographics. Following this, your matchday content will be driven by your teams' match. And finally, you can round off your matchday content by including the result of the match, some highlights, reactions, and a match recap to close off your matchday story.

What to Create

From a graphics point of view, you should split your content into four sections.

1. Pre-match
2. Matchday
3. Post-match
4. Non matchday

Pre-match

Your pre-match content should always focus on the build-up to the game. Most of your content will have a CTA [call to action] and you should promote your matches at every opportunity. As they plan their weekend, both home and away fans will need quick, relevant, and accurate information.

Your matchday build up should be planned across the week or days prior to the fixture and should include;

- **Up Next**
  - Information on the next match, including key elements such as opponents, date, kick-off time etc.

- **Match Tickets**
  - o If available, you should promote how to purchase tickets in advance and prices. If you only have cash at the gate, let everyone know and include your admission prices. Always ensure that you include a link to purchase tickets, if you have that facility available.

- **Key Info**
  - o It's good practice to make attending your ground as easy as possible for visiting and home fans. You include any travel info, parking info, when you open your ground, any food outlets and whether or not you take card payments. By sharing this information up front, you make your ground more accessible and build up a better reputation amongst visiting fans. Information can be as detailed as a full documented guide to your home ground, or a simple graphic that shows key information. Take a look at the Live Examples chapter to find out how Stenhousemuir FC take on this approach.

- **Preview**
  - o The best piece of pre-match content should come in the form of a match preview. This should be a written piece on your website, posted across your social media channels a day before your match. It can include information around the match and any history between the teams. If possible, it's good practice to include some manager and player comments. If you conduct post-match interviews from your previous match, it's good practice to ask about your next match. This will give you "free" content for your next match preview.

- **Infographic**

  An information graphic is a good piece of content to help promote the build-up to your match. There are good websites available to pick up some head-to-head stats and add a different element to your pre-match content. Depending on your level, https://www.fitbastats.com, https://www.transfermarket.com and https://www.livescores.biz are good sites for club stats.

Matchday

Your matchday content should enhance your fans' matchday experience. Although this section is labelled as 'matchday' you may have other pieces of content that you post on the actual matchday, in particular, a majority of your post-match content will also be posted on the matchday itself.

- **Matchday**
  - If you only have time to make one graphic for your matches, then it should be the Matchday graphic. Your matchday graphic is your main hook to bring supporters to the ground and should always promote a positive image with images of players celebrating, if possible. This graphic should be posted on the morning of a matchday, and a positive image will help build up some excitement for the match.

- **Starting XI**
  - The second-most important graphic is the starting line-up graphic. This will include the competition and opponent names, your numbered players and any subs, and small sponsors logos. If you plan to show your line-up in formation style, it's always best to confirm with the first team manager to make sure that

16

they are comfortable with that approach. Some managers prefer a numerical-order team, so that opposition teams do not gain even the slightest advantage.

- **Team sheet**
  - o Although not a digital comms piece, you should also prepare a printed version of the starting line-up, with opposition included, to be distributed at the ground. By taking control of this, you can ensure that it is on brand with your digital comms [although keep it easy on the colour to keep print costs down].

Post-match

Your post-match content should round up your matchday story. Although it can be tough when your team has lost, it's important to keep a consistent approach to your post-match content. While your overall tone may change depending on the match result, it's important that you continue to deliver content to your fans, win, lose or draw.

- **Match Stats**
  - o If you have the available information, you can post a match stats graphics after your match to help tell the story of the match.

- **League Table**
  - o For league games, you should post an updated league table following your match, highlighting your own club.

- **Top Scorers**
  - o As an added piece of content, you can post your top scorers for the season so far. This can be minimal and should include appearances, goals

scored and assists. This also helps you share achievements of your teams' top performers.

- **Match Report**
  - o Similar to the Match Preview, this should be a written piece that is posted on your website and then shared across your social media channels. A good match report will include a breakdown of the key moments of the match, starting line-up and subs and an indication of when subs were made, goal scorers, man of the match and attendance, if possible.

- **Match Reactions**
  - o Post-match you should always try to interview a member of the management and, if possible, a player. When choosing your player, it's important to interview someone who had a big impact on the match, but also be mindful of over-exposing the same few players to the fanbase while excluding others. It's important that you interview different players where possible.

- **Match Highlights**
  - o Match highlights are another important part of your Matchday story. A good highlights package will include line-up graphics at the start and should last no longer than 10 minutes. You can also build an extended highlight package which can include match reactions from the manager and a player.

  - o You need to know the media holdback times for your governing body. That is when you can post moving images across your digital platforms. For SPFL, this is 10pm on a Saturday and Sunday and 12am on all other days [at time of print]. Make sure you check with your own league if you're unsure.

- **Match Recap**
    - o The final piece of content for your matchday experience should be a roundup of all your activities. This can include, though not limited to; Match Report, Match Reactions, Match Highlights and Match Gallery. By having all this information in a single post, with links, you can round off your matchday story and give the fans a one-stop shop for all their matchday content.

Non matchday

You will also need to build some ad-hoc content that is not fitted to any specific match. Although there are loads of pieces you could produce, here are some examples that will give you good engagement and bring the club closer to your fans.

- **Fixtures**
    - o At the start of each month, or even week if you cover several teams [men's, women's, under 21's etc], you should post your fixtures and build up the excitement for the period ahead

- **Shop**
    - o You should promote your club shop whenever possible. The best time to sell to your fans is at the start of the season, during an international break if you have no fixtures, at Christmas and if your club is performing well and are top of the league.

- **Player Birthdays**
    - o As a member of the media team, an important part of your role will be to bring the fans and players closer together. A good way to do this is

to celebrate each player's birthday with a congratulatory post. This can be extended to engagements, weddings, births etc.

Media Shoots

For your graphics, it's important that you have your players in the latest kit, especially if you have changed kit, supplier or sponsors, and may need to do a photo shoot to capture these images.

It's most likely that you'll have three photo shoots throughout the season;

- **Main Photo Shoot**
  - This should be between pre-season and your first competitive fixture. This will give you enough content to use during your first competitive games.

- **Summer Transfer Window Close**
  - Between your main photo shoot and when the transfer window closes, you can do a mop-up photo shoot to capture any players that have signed towards the end of the transfer window.

- **January Transfer Window Close**
  - If your club signs any players in January, you should do a photo-shoot towards the end of the month to capture any players that have joined in January.

If you're at a part-time club, getting the players for a media photo shoot may prove tricky and it's important that you plan ahead and make sure you make efficient use of your time with the players.

The most important things to do when planning a media shoot;

1. Calculate how much time you will have with the players
2. Make a list of each piece of content you want to capture from each player
3. Prioritise your images to ensure that you get the most important images captured first
4. Create a plan to share with the players beforehand to ensure you use their time efficiently

You can see how we planned the Stenhousemuir media shoot in the *Live Examples* chapter.

Social Media Channels

Before we get into it, we need to look at the basics of social media including channels and account set up. This section will help you ensure that you have the basics set up for each of the social media channels that your club may benefit from. As you can use most social media channels for free, they will form the base of marketing efforts.

There are lots of social media channels that you have at your disposal. However, I recommend that you use the following as a minimum.

- **Facebook**
    - o A large percent of your audience will most likely be on Facebook and it's important that you use that channel for keeping your supporters and sponsors up to date with any information. It's unlikely that you will use Facebook for live match updates due to the algorithms that Facebook uses. They could result in live updates not being seen in chronological order, or not being seen for a few days. Facebook is useful for setting up events as well as creating two-way communication with your supporters, but it is not useful for sharing time-sensitive information.

- **Instagram**
    - o Instagram is great for sharing pictures and, in my experience, the majority of your engagement will come from this channel. Instagram Stories is an excellent way to build up your matchday content and you can even use this to tell your matchday story, with live updates. Keep in mind that an Instagram Story only lasts 15 seconds, so avoid having text-heavy content that your fans

will need to skip back to read. This will most likely see them bounce off your stories.

- **LinkedIn**
  - o LinkedIn is becoming more and more important to the commercial side of any football club. This channel allows you contact with, and market to, local businesses that could lead to sponsorship agreements. Most content on this channel will be B2B and you should use it to promote your current match sponsors, ball sponsors, kit sponsors etc. This allows potential businesses to view your brand and how strong you promote others.

- **X [Twitter]**
  - o **While its future seems to be up-in-the-air**, X will most likely be your main social media channel. From here, you can deliver breaking news, match information and updates, as well as countless other engaging content to deliver to your fans and sponsors in real time. This is most likely going to be the greatest marketing platform that you will have access to.

- **YouTube**
  - o YouTube is an important channel for your club in delivering content for your fans. By building up a strong YouTube channel, you can monetise your content as well as having tangible evidence of whether or not you are a good proposition for a local sponsor. As well as matchday highlights, you can also include manager, player and staff interviews as well as behind the scenes content that can help bring your club closer to your fans.

- **Threads**
    - ○ Threads is the newest social media platform, developed by Meta who own Facebook and Instagram. At time of writing, Threads is still in its infancy and has a long way to go before it becomes a main channel. Even if you don't plan on using Threads, create your club account to ensure that you don't lose your username.

There are other social media channels that you can use, such as TikTok, Pinterest, Blue Sky and Snapchat. While you should continue to keep an eye on their adoption rates, I would recommend having a strong presence on the top five channels listed above [Facebook, Instagram, Twitter [X], LinkedIn and YouTube], before adventuring with additional channels.

Facebook

About

Facebook provides a world-wide platform to connect with family, friends, communities and businesses. It is currently the biggest social media networking site based on global users and reach.

What Should I Post?

You should post relevant news and information as well as match information [not live updates]. You can also set up events which can be matches or fundraising events, or anything else that you'd like to remind your supporters of.

Great to post	Avoid posting
Basic Matchday information such as a matchday information graphic, Starting line-up, half-time and full-time scores	Live match updates - Facebook's algorithms won't necessarily show them to your audience in a chronological order
Events and promotional information – be sure to set up any events, such as matchday or family fun days, as proper events on Facebook as this will allow Facebook to remind your audience of the event as well as deliver key information	Any time sensitive content - Never say 'tonight' in a post, always give the date as you never know when a follower maybe seeing the content for the first time
Club news such as player signings or event information	Highlight or video packages – Always link them through to YouTube to ensure maximum engagement across duplicate channels
Club celebrations such as birthdays	
Sales posts	
Facebook Live videos – Facebook always boost their own products and by using Facebook Live to generate content, you will reach a larger audience	

When using Facebook, always be sure to tag other accounts where you can. If you're promoting a match, tag your opponents and match sponsors as this will increase the reach of your content.

Matchday Graphic - Facebook is perfect for delivering some matchday information to your fans to help tell your matchday story.

Profile Photo

Your profile photo should be 170px x 170px and should be your club crest. Ensure that it's not cropped or damaged. Your club crest is one of your biggest brand assets.

Cover Photo

Your cover photo will display at 820px x 312px on computers and 640px x 312px on smartphones. This means it's vital to find the 'sweet spot' when choosing your cover photo. Matchday images or team photos are usually best when it comes to cover photos. Stadium pictures can also work well. Make sure that your club is identifiable through your cover photo.

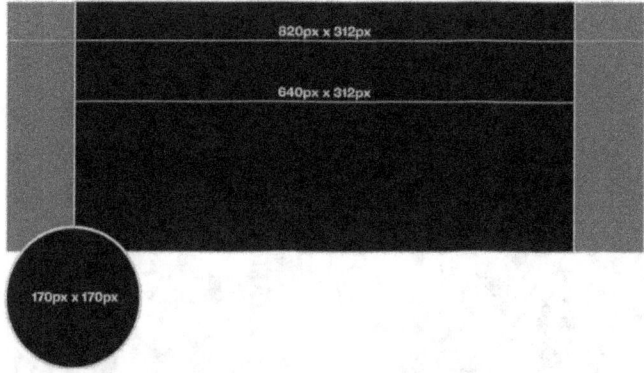

Page Name

You should keep your name consistent with your other social media channels and ensure that it's 100% clear which club you are. For example, if your club name is **Falkirk Juniors,** make sure there's no confusion with **Falkirk Amateurs**, even if the two clubs are affiliated.

About Section

This information may be more important than you think. Any information here will be picked up by search engines, so it's important that you give as much relevant information as possible. You should always include your Stadium address, website, and phone number, as well as a brief description of your club. You should look to include which competitions you take part in, when you were founded, and any other information that may be relevant.

Other Image Sizes

Regular Post Image

Images for regular posts should be 1200px x 630px.

Event Image

Images for Event Headers should be 820px x 312px.

Instagram

About

Instagram allows users to quickly share images and videos with their followers.

What Should I Post?

Instagram is all about images and video and your content should reflect this.

As well as the standard Instagram profile, Instagram also has Instagram Stories. Instagram Stories are very good at delivering a series of 'stories' to your audience and that is the perfect way to tell your matchday story in a chronological and engaging form. Your main Instagram profile can be used to deliver matchday galleries or other club information with the emphasis on photography and video content.

Instagram Stories can be great for delivering live matchday action. Unless it's a video, each story will play for 15 seconds, and all Instagram Stories will delete automatically after 24 hours.

Great to post on Instagram Stories	Avoid posting on Instagram Stories
Matchday Graphics o Team line-ups o Match updates [15-minutGre updates including half-time and full-time] o Post-match reactions	Anything with too much text o Club statements o League Tables o Match reports
Matchday Graphics with link to other channels o Match preview [linked to website] o Match highlights [linked to YouTube] o Match reactions [linked to YouTube]	
Player information – signings and birthday announcements	

Instagram Stories Up Next Graphic - Instagram stories should have enough information to enhance your matchday experience and help tell your matchday story, but it should not have so much text that it's unreadable in 15 seconds

As well as Instagram Stories, you also have your main Instagram page on which you can attach ten images per post and these will never disappear, unless deleted.

Great to post on your Instagram Page	Avoid posting on your Instagram Page
Matchday Galleries – Share unedited images on your Instagram page	Graphics – Try and keep your Instagram page to images and video only and avoid using heavily edited graphics
Video content – As well as matchday photography, you can also share video content on your Instagram page	Match Updates – There are better served channels for this type of content, and I'd keep anything matchday related away from your main Instagram page
	Anything that replies mainly on text – Content such as league tables should be left off your Instagram page. Your audience on this channel best engage with photography and videos and that's where you'll get the best engagement

Aside from matchday content, you should keep your audience engaged with other images and videos, similar to Facebook. You can also pin up to three posts on your Instagram page. You can use this to post three images that combine to show a single image.

Stenhousemuir FC's Instagram page – At Stenhousemuir, we only post matchday galleries on our main Instagram page and save everything else for Instagram Stories. We have also pinned the top three posts so that the next three months fixtures are always front and centre and immediately visible to anyone that is viewing the club's Instagram page.

Profile Photo

Your profile photo should be 110px x 110px and should be your club crest. Ensure that it's not cropped or damaged. Your club crest is one of your biggest brand assets.

Username

You should keep your name consistent with your other social media channels and ensure that it's 100% clear which club you are. For example, if your club name is **Falkirk Juniors**, make sure there's no confusion with **Falkirk Amateurs**, even if the two clubs are affiliated.

Biography

You should include which competition you play in, when you were founded and any other information that may be relevant. You can also include two links in your bio if you wish.

Image Sizes

Square Newsfeed Post

This is the image that's shown on your Newsfeed and should be 1080px x 1080px. These would usually be non-matchday images. They won't disappear unless manually deleted. You can pin images to the top of your feed for the most important content such as fixtures etc.

Instagram Stories

These are the stories that appear on the top banner in Instagram and should be 1080px x 1920px. These should primarily be matchday images as they'll disappear after 24 hours.

TOP TIP

Link your accounts!

If you have a Facebook and Instagram account, you can link these in the Meta Business Suite. By doing this, any content that you post to Instagram Stories [for example] will also post as a Facebook Reel. This will ensure you're increasing your audience size for no extra effort.

X [Twitter]

About

Twitter/X allows users to send and receive short pieces of content, usually in text and image form. Over 500 million tweets are sent out each day. In 2023 it was rebranded as X following a takeover and has since become, at times, unstable with numerous, untested, changes to the platform.

What Should I Post?

X is about delivering up-to-date information and will most likely be your primary channel for live matchday action. As well as the graphics from Instagram [resized], you should post live match updates. Don't forget to include the time and current score on all your tweets to help your supporters know that they're looking at the most up-to-date information. It's also useful to include a hashtag to allow your fans to keep track of the action.

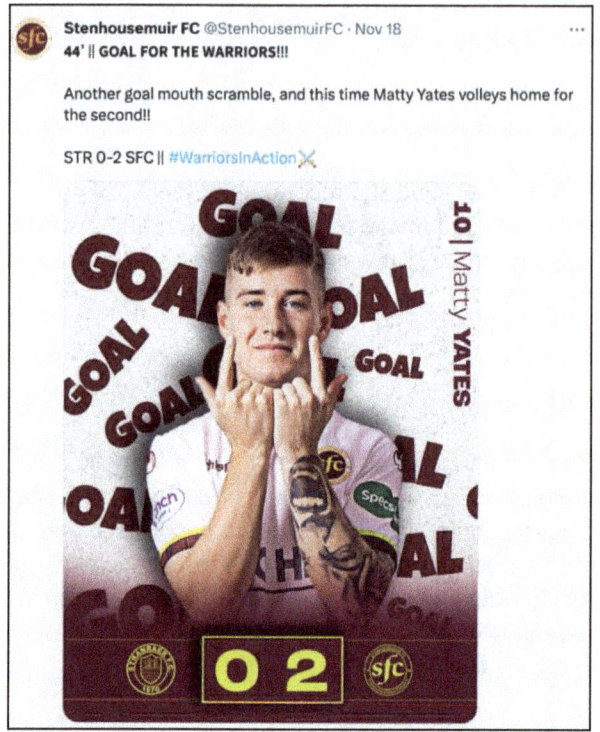

X matchday Update – You should always follow the same layout for your matchday live updates, however that looks for your club.

For Stenhousemuir, that means a bold header with time and description of the event. A brief note on the event being highlighted and then a sign off with the score and relevant hashtag.

You should also use X for breaking news and can even set up polls for your supporters to take part in.

X is great for having two-way conversations with your supporters in the correct manner [more on that later]. You can even set up live polls for your supporters to take part in.

Always remember that many users rely on accessibility features [which could include things like text readers]. If you deliver information via an image, remember to include a text version, especially with team line-ups. If you're delivering a club statement, you should always link to a website that has a text version and avoid creating a text heavy graphic.

Great to post on X	Avoid posting on X
Due to its diverse audience, the majority of your content should be posted on X, although the delivery may be different from other channels [If you're posting a sponsor post on X, your tone of voice may be a bit less formal than posting on LinkedIn]	Club statements posted as graphics – You can use a generic graphic to link to a website that holds your statement in text version
If you're posting a lot of images or videos, make sure that you're linking to a more suitable channel such as YouTube or Flickr. This makes your X profile more easy to scroll through	

Profile Photo

Your profile photo should be 400px x 400px and should be your club crest. Ensure that it's not cropped or damaged. Your club crest is one of your biggest brand assets.

Cover Photo

Your cover photo should be 1500px x 500px. Unlike Facebook, X will scale your image depending on the device used to view it. Matchday images or team photos are usually best when it comes to cover photos. Stadium pictures can also work well. Make sure that your club is identifiable through your cover photo.

Username

You should keep your name consistent with your other social media channels and ensure that it's 100% clear which club you are. For example, if your club name is **Falkirk Juniors**, make sure there's no confusion with **Falkirk Amateurs**, even if the two clubs are affiliated.

Biography

You should include which competition you play in, when you were founded or any other information that may be relevant.

Twitter/X biography - A good idea is to also highlight key information for your next match.

Image Sizes

Image Post

When posting on X, a single image should be 1200px x 675px [16:9 ratio] or 1080px x 1080px [1:1 ratio]. These sizes will show uncropped on any user's timeline.

If posting two images that aren't 1:1 ratio, X will crop both, while retaining an overall 16:9 aspect ratio. X's algorithm looks for text in your image and will crop based on this, so you'll never really know where your picture will be cropped. You could post the same two images twice, and X will crop them differently each time.

If you post two images that are 1:1 ratio then both will be shown in full, albeit with a scaled down version.

If posting three images, X will show two at 16:9 ratio and the third will be show at 1:1, regardless of the picture sizes.

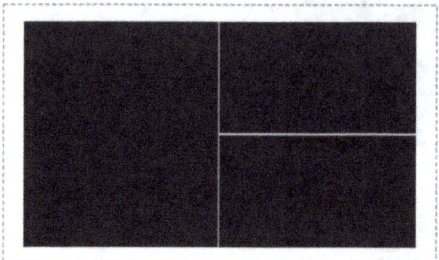

If posting four images, X will show all four at 16:9 ratio regardless of the picture sizes.

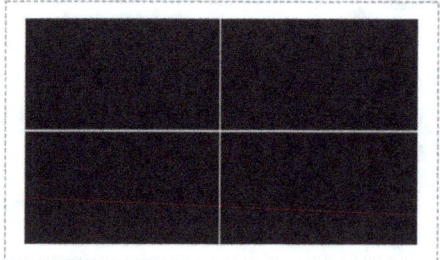

Carousels

Carousel Ads allows you to drive people to a specific link through multiple images or videos — all within a single post.

You can include up to six images or videos per post, each with their own link. Or, you can have one single link for each image or video. You can use a 1:1 or 16:9 ratio. However, every video and image used in a single carousel must be the same ratio.

At Stenhousemuir, we have a pinned carousel tweet that promotes the season's new kits. This allows any person on the Stenhousemuir FC X page to swipe along the six images.

LinkedIn

About

LinkedIn allows users to network with professionals in their fields for personal or professional gain. It can also be used for establishing B2B relationships.

What Should I Post?

LinkedIn will help you to attract new sponsors to your club, as well as add value to your current sponsors. When looking for sponsors, you can post and attach a commercial brochure or graphic to help hook potential partners. It's also good practice to promote your current sponsors through this channel. Successes here can be used as leverage when attracting new sponsors or renewing current sponsorship deals.

Sponsorship Post – LinkedIn is a great way to support current, and attract new, sponsors. If you have a matchday sponsor, be sure to give them a LinkedIn post and tag them to allow maximum exposure and help towards a repeat deal.

If you perform any community or charity work, it's also good to promote your events and successes on LinkedIn. Companies will be more likely to partner with you if you have a positive community impact.

If you have a charity aspect to your club, companies will be keen to partner with you if it helps their CSR targets [Corporate Social Responsibility].

Great to post on LinkedIn	Avoid posting on LinkedIn
Sponsor announcements, either new club or shirt sponsors, or matchday sponsor	Any matchday content that doesn't pertain to a sponsor
Any local community content that helps shine a light on your club and could attract new sponsors or income streams	Any club news that doesn't drive any potential commercial revenue [such as a player's birthday]
A new player signing is always good to post on LinkedIn, especially if you're looking for player sponsors.	

Profile Photo

Your profile photo should be 400px x 400px and should be your club crest. Ensure that it's not cropped or damaged. Your club crest is one of your biggest brand assets.

Cover Photo

Your cover photo should be 1128px x 191px. Unlike Facebook, LinkedIn will scale your image dependent on the device used to view it. Matchday images or team photos are usually best when it comes to cover photos. Stadium pictures can also work well. Make sure that your club is identifiable through your cover photo.

Username

You should keep your name consistent with your other social media channels and ensure that it's 100% clear which club you are. For example, if your club name is **Falkirk Juniors**, make sure there's no confusion with **Falkirk Amateurs**, even if the two clubs are affiliated.

Headline

You should include which competition you play in, when you were founded and any other information that may be relevant.

Summary

Here you have 2,000 characters to promote your club. You should strike a balance between being general enough to cover your key information and specific enough to show up on search engines. As users will see the first 220 characters before having to click to 'view more,' you should make sure those first characters are interesting.

Image Sizes

Image Post

A LinkedIn image should be 1200px x 628px. You can also post images at 1200px x 1200px which will view uncropped on a desktop but will be cropped to 1200px x 628px when viewing on a mobile device.

Medium Term – Take Your Content to the Next Level

Social Media Engagement

This section will introduce you to the role of social media in today's society and how you can use it to develop your club's relationship with fans and club partners.

The growth of social media

Social media has become an integral part of modern-day life across the world. We're better connected than ever, with half of the world's population considered to be active social media users. Smartphone usage continues to rise and there are now believed to be over five billion unique smartphone users worldwide.

As the world spends more and more time on social media platforms, you should take the opportunity to be a part of the conversations and add value to your supporters' lives. This will spread awareness of your club and drive valuable actions, such as engagement, data capture and [hopefully] sales.

However, as social media has become such an established media channel, the rules of engagement have moved on and not all clubs have caught up. Your objective on social media is to deliver value to anyone that discovers your content.

While your posts don't always have to be about the club they should almost NEVER be about the people that manage your accounts. This is not what people want, and you'll lose out on proper engagement.

To attract interest in your club, your content should be either useful or entertaining. You can deliver the information that your audience seeks, or you can entertain them by sharing media that fascinates, amuses or tells a story.

How can social media benefit your club?

Social media will only benefit your club when it has a **positive effect** on the relationship between the club and your fans and partners.

A social media success gap is building between clubs that use social media in an informal, ad-hoc way and those who take a more planned and strategic approach. Many of the larger clubs have fully documented social media plans and strategies as they have employees who are paid to do so. Clubs at lower levels will, most likely, require volunteers to give up their time to build and manage these strategies and this is a difficult position to fulfil. However, you should never be scared to ask for help. If there's a college or university nearby, reach out for students to get some first-hand experience. Your club will only benefit from it.

Making social media a priority will help clubs to:

Improve your club's brand recognition and authority.

More and more people are discovering new clubs on social media. The more mentions and interactions you attract, the more authoritative your club becomes.

Improve club loyalty.

Any football fan that follows your clubs on social media is, by definition, interested in your club. Those that engage by sharing and replying tend to be more loyal, and fans of your club. Social media is also a great supporter service channel that gives you the chance to improve your club's reputation.

Move fans and sponsors along the path to purchase.

Keeping your club at the front of your fans and sponsors [or potential sponsors] minds will increase the chance that they'll think of your club the next time they're looking to purchase anything that your club sells, or services that you offer.

It's easy to think that this may be limited to kits and merchandise for fans, but you should also consider things like lotteries and fundraising initiatives for non-fans or even services for local residents. For instance, does your club run a cafe during the week, or offer pitch hire? Maybe a once-a-month reminder would be of interest to those in the local community who aren't necessarily fans. And then once they are following your social media accounts, it makes it easier to try to bring them along to a game or two.

And for sponsors, these types of exposure may help convince them to extend current deals or increase their sponsorship standing within the club.

Improve sponsorship opportunities.

Potential sponsors will turn to social media to help them decide how much value your club could be to them. If you have a large, engaged, audience, your club could become very attractive to local businesses.

Increase web traffic.

Inbound traffic and getting good links to your website is very desirable, especially when directed to a club shop or ticket sales. Social media is an effective way for people to find and share content.

Good performance in this area should also improve your SEO [search engine optimisation] rankings, moving your content higher up in the search engine results. So if you have pitches to hire, your club could be the top result on Google for pitch hire in your area.

Understand your fans better.

Social media allows your club to communicate with your fans and sponsors in real time. Don't be scared to talk to your fans and interact with them, in the correct manner. You'll be amazed at how valuable their views can be to your club.

By keeping an on your engagement across your social media channels, you can read what your fans are looking for. Perhaps they like a piece of content that another club has done – can you create similar content? Don't be scared to copy other clubs, they'll be ready to copy you too.

Create communities.

Social media allows your club, and individuals, to create digital communities across your channels with a shared interest, or goal. By creating your own communities, you can become more accessible than ever to your fans, which will help build that loyalty.

If there are football forums, make sure you take part in the discussions and answer any questions that you can. This adds an extra channel to your output. Always remember though that you're the voice of your club and never engage in any arguments across any digital channels. Sometimes it's better to say nothing.

Paid vs Organic

You'll probably never use paid social media activity, but it's useful to have some basic knowledge around paid and organic content.

ORGANIC social media is content with no paid support. This is where you post an update and let the social media companies decide where and how other people see your message.

PAID social media is when you pay a platform to place an advert or 'boost' your content to your targeted audience.

Normally, your fanbase will already follow you, so you will be able to deliver content to that group without paying. However, if you're looking at wider events, such as fundraising, sponsorship searches or anything that's beneficial to non-supporters of your club, you may wish to explore paid content and target local residents.

Organic

Engagement on organic posts will vary significantly based on how relevant and interesting the social media company's algorithm deems your content to be. Even the best and most engaged clubs will struggle to reach all, or even most, of their existing follower base with only organic content.

If you're not planning and creating the correct content, you may only reach about 6% [average estimated reach per post] of your followers. Remember that the people that you want to reach with organic content will be your most engaged fans. This type of content that serves the informational needs of your existing fanbase is often referred to as '**help**' content.

Paid Advertising

Alongside your organic content, there are also opportunities to pursue your social media objectives through paid advertising content. This is a completely different approach as you can target a far wider audience. Though this means you can target non-fans of the club, you should ensure that the content delivered in this method is appealing enough to engage with this group.

For example, in June 2020 Clyde FC promoted their '**Be an Owner**' initiative which appealed to all football fans and not those exclusive to the Club. Paid advertising would have allowed them to target a larger audience that normally wouldn't have seen, or engaged with, their content. If Clyde felt that the money spent on paid advertising would lead to a positive ROI [return on investment], then they could've run some digital ads.

Creating a Fan-Centric Strategy

This section will give you an overview of the concepts of social media strategy, supporter's needs and wants, loyalty in social media and the importance of raising engagement.

The foundations of a successful strategy

Regardless of who your social media content is targeted towards, it should be of value to the people that it is shown to.

To achieve this, make sure that you're clear on the following;

- **Your clubs' purpose** – ethos, ethics and reason to exist
- **Your audience** – interests, motivations, age, location, demographics data, media habits
- **Your objectives** – SMART social media objectives

These three things will form the foundation of your strategy. Ensure that you have a clear, documented strategy that defines; who you are, who you're talking to, and why. This will help make sure that your content remains relevant and engaging.

Your platform strategy

This vital document will make sure that you've understood where your fans spend their time thinking about your club, and how they prefer to engage. You can then define which platforms your club will put resources into and what you will do to interact with those fans on each platform.

Your strategy will identify different groups of audiences across your channels.

For example,
LinkedIn = Sponsors and Partners
Instagram = Players
Twitter/X = Fans

[remember that this is a guide, and there will be overlap between channels]

This framework will help you to share your club message with different people in different ways, while staying true to your club's overall values.

Your content plan is a detailed document which defines your club at a granular level. Think about how your messaging will communicate all the things you want your audience to believe, feel, or think about your club. It should be clear to anyone picking it up internally, how each of your club's core brand values should be articulated in your social media content.

Your plan will also include a timeline or calendar so this messaging can be planned in the context of the season, covering any topical events and key club moments.

This and all other strategy documents should be:

● Owned by one specific person – it will be their job to keep it up to-date
● Available to anyone in the club, at any time [Likely hosted on Google Docs or Dropbox].

Social media channel strategy template

The purpose of this template is to plan your social media strategy for the year, aligning your social media activity with your club's goals.

Objectives

Club Goal	Marketing objective	Social SMART objectives	KPIs

A basic template can be found here - bit.ly/FootballMarketing

Deepening your relationships through content

To stay at the front of your supporter's mind, it's important to become their trusted source of information for everything about your club.

Like any other kind of human relationship, this bond is deepened through mutually exchanged values. It's kept open by good faith on both sides.

- Be strategic
- Create value
- Experiment and take appropriate creative risks
- Stay true to your club's values

Social Media Objectives

In this section, we'll look at how social media can contribute to your club's main objectives. This will help you build the foundation that you need to create an effective campaign strategy.

Setting the right social media objectives for success

It's crucial to be able to articulate your core club goals as social media objectives. This will help you plan your content and ensure that your activity is aligned and integrated with the club.

Social media objectives are derived from marketing objectives, which in turn, are derived from the goals of the club.

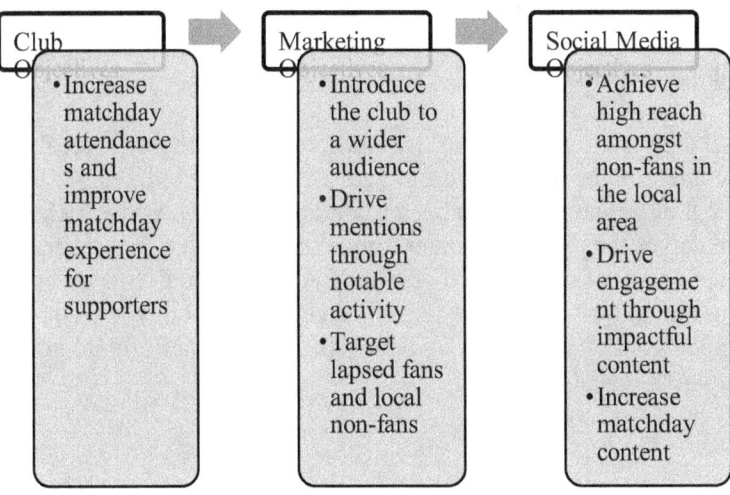

Club	Marketing	Social Media
• Increase matchday attendances and improve matchday experience for supporters	• Introduce the club to a wider audience • Drive mentions through notable activity • Target lapsed fans and local non-fans	• Achieve high reach amongst non-fans in the local area • Drive engagement through impactful content • Increase matchday content

The above diagram shows a club objective as the starting point. The marketing team should use it as a base for the development of their own objectives. Each relevant department in the club should also set their own objectives based on the overall club objective.

In contribution to the set marketing objectives, the social media manager will develop the social strategy with its own connected objectives. These will be specific to social media but will be fully integrated with the marketing goals and, in turn, the club's main objective.

Club objectives will be specific to your club, based on size and skills and knowledge of people involved with the club.

Your club's objectives may be consumed by the following areas;*

Club awareness

For 'top of the funnel' marketing, social media plays a vital role. Video is becoming more and more popular regarding awareness building. Video lends itself well to capturing attention, explaining new concepts, and introducing new information to a defined audience.

In the wider business world, brands will create highly shareable content in the hope that customers' first contact with their brand will be something that's been shared by a friend. As the friend receives the piece of content from a trusted source, this leverages the power of online word of mouth. Although you're never likely to attract new 'hardcore' fans through this method, you could open your club to a new audience that could benefit future non-football events.

EXERCISE

Have a think about your content, whether it be a social media post, an email, or any other digital comms.
- Is it share-worthy? Would you send it to a friend?
- How many pieces of content like this have you seen from other clubs and have shared it, is there any opportunities for you to create something similar?

Data capture

Even at a lower-level football club, it's important that you have proprietary supporter data.
This allows you to have readily available information and make sure that you do not rely solely on a single site social media to store your customer lists, or to deliver club messages.

Social media can be used to build a database, be it supporters' information [B2C or Business To Customer] or sponsorship and partnership information [B2B or Business to Business]. This data can then be used to send out newsletters or information on season ticket sales, kit launches etc.

If you are collecting data, please ensure that you're up to date on your country's latest data regulations. For Europe, you can visit the ICO's helpful page **here.** In the United States, there's no federal-level statute like the GDPR, but states have adopted their own legislation, most notably the CCPA in California. You can read about GDPR variations around the world **here**.

Sales

Traditionally, social media managers have avoided tying their activity to commercial goals. Developing a social community will always be a long-term and indirect form of marketing and shouldn't be expected to be a quick win. However, the increasingly algorithm driven social landscape has decreased organic audience.

This lends itself back to data capture where you can be more confident of targeting your club's fans correctly when delivering an important sales message. Monthly newsletters and email bulletins can help fulfil this.

*These examples are purely aligned to marketing. Your club will likely have other objectives which may not require marketing and social media support.

Objectives and KPIs

Each of your social media objectives should refer to at least one KPI [Key Performance Indicator] – a metric that's measurable and determines success. Choose KPIs that will best determine success.

For example, if you have an objective of 'growing your clubs audience', that could mean the following;

- Grow social reach among 18-35 year old males in your local town
- Grow the club's overall social media following
- Grow the engagement of your social media content

My 3 Recommended KPIs

Here are three key social media KPIs which I recommend will move your club forward.

It's helpful to divide them to make sure that you serve all of these areas of your social media activity.

KPIs 1 - Growth

KPIs that describe growth of your social audience and reach, such as:

- Followers
- Likes
- Views or impressions
- Reach of content

These could be used as follows:

- **Club Objective**: Introduce the club to new potential sponsors in the local area
- **Marketing Objective**: Build awareness of the club amongst local businesses
- **Social Media Objective**: Gain LinkedIn post reach of 100,000 among local business before the end of the season

KPIs 2 - Interaction

Metrics that quantify interaction with your brand on social media platforms, such as:

- Likes
- Comments
- Shares
- Mention of club / Hashtag

These could be used as follows:

- **Club Objective**: Grow Season Ticket retention
- **Marketing Objective**: Develop a community around current season ticket holders
- **Social Media Objective**: Grow likes and comments on our Facebook and Instagram, posts by 10% MoM [month on month] for the next 12 months

KPIs 3 - Impact

Once the above objectives are in place, you can measure the impact of your social activity on the club itself. This will help you quantify the ROI [return on investment] of your social media activity.

Examples

- Website traffic from social media channels
- Club shop conversions from social media channels
- Season Ticket sales
- New sponsorship partnerships

These could be used as follows:

- **Club Objective**: Increase replica kit sales
- **Marketing Objective**: Reach supporters or kit enthusiasts worldwide and ensure that they have access to purchasing a replica kit
- **Social Media Objective**: Generate 1,000 conversions from social media content during the two weeks launch period

Choose the right metrics to measure success

This section will look at understanding how social media fits into the supporter relationship journey and what key metrics will best support you in your quest to help them. It will also help you to make informed decisions about which metrics will strengthen relationships with your club.

Understanding social media metrics

Social media can drive value at all stages of the supporter journey and it's important to understand which metrics deserve your focus. The decision on which metrics to use should be based on your wider objectives.

For example, with a kit launch, the supporter journey, and metrics used, may look like this:

- **Awareness** – *"I know the club is releasing a new kit today."*
  - o Reach
  - o Impressions
  - o Views
- **Consideration** – *"I'm likely to buy the new kit sometime."*
  - o Likes
  - o Comments
  - o Interactions
- **Conversion** – *"I'm buying the new kit today."*
  - o Clicks
  - o Conversions
- **Loyalty & Advocacy** – *"I want more people to know about this kit."*
  - o All of the above
  - o Shares

The metrics on key social media channels are very similar and can often be grouped together [likes, comments etc.]. However, their meaning and value are often not directly comparable. For example, a like on Instagram happens in a different context, via a different platform and for different reasons than a like on Facebook.

Similarly, non-social media metrics such as conversion and website traffic are difficult to compare between channels as they work differently to retain users.

Let's look at a broad hierarchy for categories of metrics.

1. **Shares / Reposts**
   This is the Holy Grail. Shares and reposts are used by supporters to share and recommend your club's messages with their own followers. On social media, shares are key to driving club awareness and supporter engagement. If a follower is sharing your content then it will be seen by people who aren't following you

2. **Comments / Replies**
   The best social media content is about provoking conversations [in a positive way]. Comments are a strong indicator that you have engaging content. It's also a good sign that you're nurturing a social community around your club.

3. **Likes / Favourites**
   This feedback lets you know when your content has been positively received and is making an impact. Likes will often lead to higher rates of engagement.

4. **Reach**
   This is a record of the number of people who have seen your post and will be driven by your levels of engagement. This will show you how many people you are reaching organically with your content.

Followers – a vanity metric!

You may notice that followers are not on this list.

While it may seem obvious that a large number of followers will increase your reach, a large group of unengaged followers will damage your ability to have genuinely engaging content. As discussed in an earlier chapter, not everyone will see your content when you post. If your posts are delivered to non-engaged followers [who will never engage], then it will rarely be seen by your most engaged followers.

For example, imagine you have 1,000 followers. 20% are supporters and 80% non-supporters. There's a very low chance that your actual supporters will see your content. Remember, it's estimated that, on average, only 6% of your followers will see a piece of organic [not paid] content. Therefore, it's better to have just 200 followers who are genuine supporters than 1,000 followers, of whom only 20% are engaged supporters.

When more people engage with your content, you will achieve a higher reach.

Key social media metrics

At the time of publication, Facebook, Instagram and Twitter/X are currently the three most used social media channels in the UK. So, let's look at the key measures on each of these platforms. Be aware that, despite having the same or similar names, the actual meanings of the measures do differ.

Twitter / X

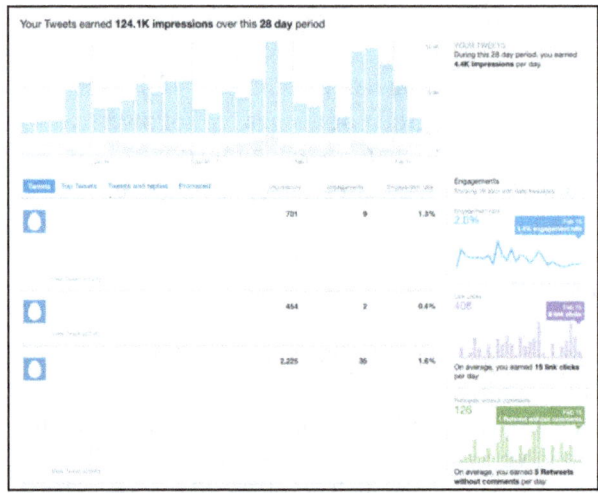

Reposts [formerly Retweets]

This is the same as the 'share' function on Facebook and it puts another user's posts into the sharee's timeline. This is the best opportunity that you have of getting your organic content into the eyes of users that do not follow you. Receiving reposts of your posts is a driver of visibility on X and the strongest sign of engagement.

Impressions

The most prominent metric to view in X is impressions. This is the number of times that a specific content has been viewed. This is not limited to your followers. The more that your followers engage with your content, the more impressions it will have.

Mentions

This is known as the 'earned social media' in its purest form. A mention on X is of great value to your club.

A mention is [almost always] public, so therefore can be seen and searched for on, as well as off of, X. A mention can also be monitored by software which tracks the mentions and the sentiment of the language around them thus providing valuable context to the raw data.

Likes

A more recent engagement type on the platform. Likes allow users to respond positively to a post without putting that concept on their feed. A like suggests a post was valuable in some way to the end user and can increase visibility due to the algorithm prioritising popular content.

Facebook

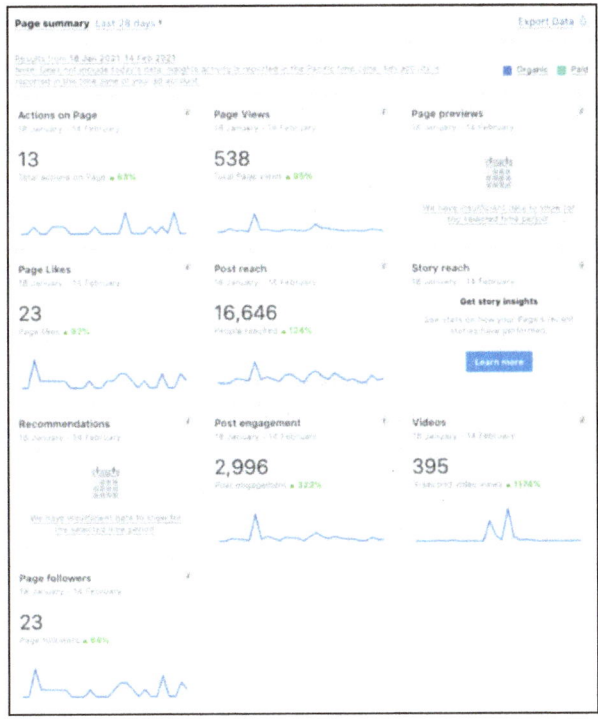

Reactions [formerly likes]

A range of reactions – angry, sad etc., through which users can express their response with some emotional dimension. The different reaction types do not technically have different relative values, though can point to customer sentiment [eg. 'love' vs 'angry']

Engagement rates

This metric refers to the aggregate number of people who have engaged in any way with your post. This could be a reaction, a comment, a share, a click etc. The metric is expressed as a percentage of everyone reached.

Reach [page or post]

In light of declining organic reach, this is now the most accurate measurement of your audience size. When referring to pieces of content, these numbers encompass both users who saw the result of organic and of paid activity. This distinction is usually made clear in the insights and analytics tools.

Page Likes

Those who 'like' a Facebook page subscribe to posts from that page. However, in recent years organic reach has declined sharply, meaning that just because someone has liked your page, doesn't mean they will be exposed to your content.

Shares

A less frequently used engagement feature is Facebook's share functionality. This is only likely to be used with truly viral content, and so is a key measure in these campaigns where organic spread of the content is the key objective. If a follower shares your content, it has a very high chance that it will be seen by a non-follower and therefore widen your reach.

Comments

Of the key channels, Facebook has arguably the most cohesive threading of discussion within comments, allowing users to more easily see a comment in the wider context of others.

Comments are, as on any channel, are a higher level of engagement than single-click reactions as they denote higher emotional investment, and also elicit further discussion from other users, helping to build a genuine community around your club.

Instagram

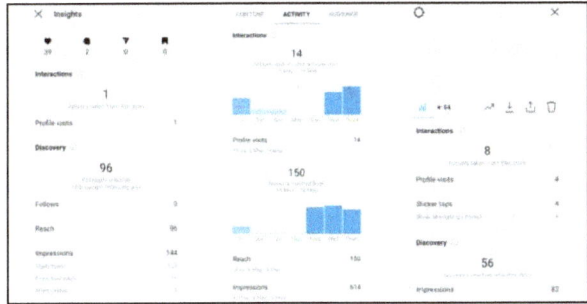

Likes

This tends to be the first metric you should look at on Instagram. But, given the Instagram culture of liking, this doesn't necessarily reflect on high levels of engagement.

Stories

Instagram stories have some separate metrics. For those pieces of content, the interactions metric also includes replies and sticker taps. Additionally, navigation statistics are provided, which detail instances where a user tapped backwards and forwards in your story; tapped to the next account's story; and exited your story.

Impressions

The total number of times a piece of content has been viewed.

Reach

The number of users that have seen your post or story.

Interactions

Engagements of any sort on a post or story. This includes profile visits.

Comments

Comments are a strong indication of engagement on Instagram.

Comments, which can be positive or negative, indicate a higher level of emotional engagement. If you're looking to grow a community around your online content [which you should be] then growing levels of comments are a great indicator.

EXCERCISE

Using the above information, take a look at the analytics sections on your social media channels
- Are there any channels that perform better than others in terms of reach?
- Do your pictures get a better rate of engagement on Instagram than on Twitter/X?
- What channel has the highest engagement rate?
  - The engagement rate is calculated as the total number of interactions your content receives

divided by your total number of followers, multiplied by 100%

Final thoughts

Social media companies are always enhancing their analysis as they become more relevant to a user than ever before.

If you're able to afford a monthly subscription, I would recommend a website such as *Publer* or *Hootsuite* that will offer an analytics package to make it even easier to pull out key metrics to allow you to grow your marketing strategies.

Use the SMART objective framework

It is important that everyone at your club sets objectives that work together in one direction towards the club's overall goals or marketing objectives. The SMART objective framework is the most widely accepted method to achieve this result.

SMART is an acronym for: **Specific, Measurable, Achievable, Realistic** and **Timed.**

Specific - Direct and unambiguous description of the outcome

The more specific an objective is, the more you'll be able to focus on it and the more likely your success will be. Try answering the five 'W' questions - Who, What, Where, Why, and Which. These can really help to reach a useful level of specificity.

Measurable – Quantifiable in plain numbers

For an objective to be useful, you need to know if you achieved it. How exactly will you measure the success of your activity? Think about the metrics you'll need to obtain, and how you'll get them.

Achievable – Realistically do-able within practical and resource constraints

It's great to have ambitious goals. But for the digital and social media campaigns that contribute to your wider business clubs, you must have realistic aims. We must make sure that you have the requisite resources, budget, skills and time to achieve them.

Relevant – Objectives that contribute to the wider business aims

A relevant objective is one that is directly derived from, and aligned with, wider marketing or club goals. Does it drive forward those broader aims? Is it the right time for this?

Timed – Built around a specific timeline

Quite simply, every objective needs a deadline.

What do SMART Objectives look like?

When you make your objective SMART, you turn something like this:

"Sell more season tickets".

… into something like this:

"Sell 1,000 Season Tickets, with 80% of those sales before our first home game".

While both objectives tell a team or person what to do, and can ultimately achieve the same outcome, the SMART version gives very clear instruction and parameters.

By quantifying the goal, we get a sense of how much work there is to do and will be able to gauge progress towards that. And a deadline provides a timeframe in which to plan our activity.

Tips for goal setting

- Describe outcomes not activities - rather than aiming to 'Livestream a Friday Manager Interview', define a solid outcome such as 'attract 500 weekly viewers of our live-streamed Manager Interview'.

- Avoid objectives which maintain a status quo - such as 'post on Twitter/X every day'. These are unlikely to inspire and distract from your more ambitious, important goals.

- Weed out any ambiguity in the wording of your objectives. It should be clear to anyone whether or not that goal was achieved, without the need for subjective opinion or judgement.

- Make sure objectives, activities and results are freely available within the club. For instance, if you set an objective around social engagement, create a universally readable report at the end of the timeframe and put it in a place where club employees can access it, e.g. Google Drive, without reliance on you, or a colleague, to offer-up information.

Social Media Content Planning

In this section, you will see the principles of good content marketing and what you should include in a content plan when setting it up.

The principles of good content marketing

Content marketing works by creating and using content to deliver profitable supporter interactions.
As content is used to drive interaction, it should always have a purpose for the club and a value for the target audience.

There are, broadly, six forms of high-value content:

- **Entertainment** - Engaging content that is enjoyable to consume.
- **Conviction** - Persuasive content that presents compelling ideas.
- **Inspiration** - Unusual and motivating content that sparks something new.
- **Information** - Sharing knowledge and building authority.
- **Education** - 'How to' content that teaches the user.
- **Support** - Demonstrating care/ providing a helping hand.

The consumer challenge for content marketers

The way football fans find content has been transformed. Many fans are now using digital channels as their go-to place for news and information, with search engines and social platforms being the most popular. The way content is viewed has also dramatically changed over time, with fans more likely to spend more time on video and social posts, than longer forms of content and blogs.

This changes the costs, skills, and timescales of content creation and needs to be taken into account when planning and executing a content strategy.

For your club's social media efforts to be successful, you must be well organised and guided by one centrally located, methodically planned, content calendar.

With multiple internal and external contributors and stakeholders, unmanaged social media pages can become a free-for-all broadcast of promotional content. This is why the most proficient clubs who operate in social media are highly protective of their publishing guidelines.

If you need to manage contributors, it is possible to find a variety of collaborative online tools that will help maintain a central editor function to approve each post. However, a spreadsheet hosted on a platform such as Google Drive will work just as well.

What to include in your content plan?

When planning your upcoming content, make sure your content is tightly integrated with the rest of your marketing activities.

Your first considerations should be your club's key events, milestones and any campaigns that will require your support. It is in your interest to proactively discuss with your team how you can support their work. This will protect your channels from becoming too promotional and ultimately running the risk of losing your audience's attention.

Include topical moments

Research key holidays and special days, as well as cultural events such as major TV shows, film and music releases. Fathers' Day and Mothers' Day should always be in your planner.

However, you should be careful. While it is tempting to pad out your marketing with "easy content" national Event Days, all of these topical moments should be considered in light of your club's core values and club / marketing objectives, as well as the relevance to your target audience.

Likewise, many cultural events are potentially hazardous for clubs to create content around. Political events such as elections, or anniversaries of controversial historical figures. If you're not sure, then don't include it in your plans.

Plan both cross-channels and channel specific

Ensure your campaigns are communicated across your relevant platforms. Your output must clearly come from a consistent and integrated club. Achieving this consistency can make sure that each of your platforms has its own specific content plan, allowing content to be tailored to each specific platform.

For example, if you're looking to hire a volunteer videographer, your approach on X or Facebook, will be different to that on LinkedIn. This is down to your audience in each channel. For LinkedIn, you will deliver a more technical, professional post. Whereas on X or Facebook, you may be a bit more light hearted and fun with your post.

Hashtags

Hashtags started as a tagging convention, whereby a '#' symbol is placed before a keyword and included in a post to make it discoverable by a relevant audience. It is now integrated into most social platforms.

Originating on X as a community convention, it was then implemented into the platform as a feature a couple of years later. Since then, it has continued to grow and is now the standard means by which people tag content on most platforms.

This being said, usage and value of hashtags vary across social media platforms. On X, for example, they are primarily used to connect in-the-now content and you should look to capitalise on these opportunities, where they are relevant.

Instagram users, on the other hand, make different use of hashtags. Here they are used to order content in its thematic context, denoting the topics and interests of the content. Fashion, food, travel, design and fitness are some of the most popular topics.

There are two key uses of hashtags that you should use across all your channels.

- **Your clubs' hashtags** – You should have a few hashtags specifically for your club.
    - o **Live match** – This should be a hashtag that you use when commenting on a live match. For Stenhousemuir FC, this is *#WarriorsInAction*
    - o **Community** – If you have a community or charity aspect to your club, you can also have a specific hashtag when talking about the community or charity aspects. For Stenhousemuir FC, this is *#WarriorsTogether*
    - o **Other Teams** – If you have multiple teams across your club and you're communicating with or cross-promoting, you should pull in a specific hashtag to use across all clubs and accounts when interacting with another. For Stenhousemuir FC, this is *#WarriorsAsOne*

- **Trending hashtags** – By keeping an eye on current trends, you should capitalise on trending hashtags by using them in your content when appropriate. This could be a random event, or be a dated event, such as *Show Racism the Red Card* [#SRtRC] or *Rainbow Laces* [#RainbowLaces]. By using these hashtags, your content

Remember to utilise hashtags across your channels to maximise the reach to your target audience and be visible to people that don't follow your club.

How to set up your plan

Now that you know some of the basics, it's time to set up your plan.

I highly recommend that you create your content plan in a calendar format, so that you can always refer back to what you did on each platform and when you did it. This will also speed up your reporting and analysis process.

In this content plan template, I've set up the basic information: date, platform, and posting time. You can access this template at http://bit.ly/37jKGId.

Date	Social Network	Time	Content Type	Sub-Topic	Social Copy	Character Count	External Link	Asset File Location	Notes
	Facebook					0			
						0			
						0			
						0			
	Instagram					0			
						0			
						0			
						0			
01-Jan	Twitter					0			
						0			
						0			
						0			
	LinkedIn					0			
						0			
						0			
						0			

Once you have your template, you can then go into more detailed planning.

Content type

As discussed above, content must be varied, with different content types working best on different channels. Use your analysis to understand the frequency of each type on each platform, then set this up as a predetermined structure to follow. This will help you when brainstorming what to include in each post.

Sub-Topic

This should be aligned with the right audience on the right channels.

Social Copy

"Copy" is a fancy marketing term for "Words" or "Content."

The Copy column should contain the actual copy which will be posted, including #tags, @references etc. The idea is for the copy to be signed off here, then copied and pasted into the relevant platform.

Character count

Character count in some platforms is limited, while in others you will find that certain character lengths will be more effective.

- **Facebook character limits**
  - **Username** – at least 5 characters and up to 50 characters
  - **Page Description** – 255 Characters
  - **Facebook comments** – 8,000 characters

- **Instagram character limits**
  - **Username** – 30 characters
  - **Bio** – 150 characters
  - **Headline** – 40 characters

- o **Body text** – 125 characters
- o **Link description** - 30 characters
- o **Captions** – 2,200 characters
  - ▪ Although you can use 2,200 characters, it's not recommended as huge blocks of text can look messy and distract your audience from the main focus of your post. The ideal length is 1-50 characters

- **Twitter/X character limits**
  - o **Twitter/X handle** – 15 characters
  - o **Username** – 50 characters
  - o **Bio** – 160 characters
  - o **DMs** – 10,000 characters
  - o **Tweets / Posts** – 280 characters
    - ▪ 280 limit is for regular accounts, if you're a X Premium / Twitter Blue subscriber, you will have a tweet character limit of 25,000

- **LinkedIn character limits**
  - o **Company page name** – 100 characters
  - o **Company update** – 700 characters
  - o **Post headline** - 100 characters
  - o **Content length** – 110,000 characters

- **YouTube character limits**
  - o **Video title** – 100 characters
  - o **YouTube description** – 5,000 characters
  - o **Playlist titles** – 150 characters
  - o **YouTube tags** – 500 character total

External link

This is where your social post will link to, for example to the club shop, new item, or partner web page, etc...

Asset file location

"Assets" are the supporting images, videos, documents, or audio clips that will accompany your content.

Put a direct link through to any assets in its location, this will ensure that the person posting has the correct video or image, as well as the right, signed-off, version. This can be linked to Google Drive

Notes

Any notes about the post can go in here – for example, if you have intentionally tried something different, the piece of content is part of a test, or perhaps you need to inform a third party or sponsor when the content goes Live.

Implementing your plan

You should decide who within your team is responsible for completing each column; who should do the final check to ensure all the information is correct, and who will be posting or scheduling the item.

This will help the plan run more smoothly.

For smaller clubs, a single person may be responsible for each aspect of this planner. In this case, a planner is still 100% necessary. It will give an insight into your social media plan, make it easier for you to create content in the future, or even to hand over social accounts to someone else [should you wish to take a step back].

Reactive and planned social media content development

In this section, we'll look at the concepts of planned and reactive content and learn how to effectively brief your creative producers and plan the content creation.

Planned Content

Like any publisher, social media is most relevant and interesting to your fans and audience when you offer a blend of thoughtfully produced content that meets their informational or entertainment needs.

The content should be topical and bring them your club's relevant news and talking points, filtered through your unique lens. While there is no golden ratio for planned vs reactive content, there is a well-tested process for managing these various creative processes in your club.

Firstly, your Content Plan should plot your content strategy each month. This may be a month in advance depending on the scale of your club and content ambitions. Obviously your matchday information will be supplemented on top of this activity and should continue ongoing, regardless.

If you plan a month in advance, the process will look like this:

1ˢᵗ day of the month

- Review last month's content performance
- Identify the best and worst performing content
- Find what specific factors contributed to their results

1st week of the month

- Brainstorm and define your content for next month

- Start with key topical moments and brand moments
- Fill in with evergreen [less topical] content as necessary
- Plot every individual planned post in your content calendar
- Create your content brief from this, defining exactly what visual media, copy and technical production must happen, when and by whom

Weeks 2-4 of the month

- Creative production of all of the briefed content
- Ideally, you will have most of the content produced before the month begins, though some larger pieces might need more time
- Ensure your content is ready a week ahead of publishing

The month of content publishing

Every day, the staff / volunteers responsible for posting or scheduling content should refer to the calendar and publish accordingly.

Bigger campaigns, of course, may require more lead time than one month, but your regular planned content should follow this straight-forward process.

Reactive Content

While planned content is your "bread and butter," you should always keep one eye out for any events that allow your club to put its unique spin on the events of the day [or even minute].

This Reactive Content can lead to some of the most spectacular results if done well, but it can also be fraught with risks.

Risks and benefits

The risks associated with Reactive Content are numerous, and several things can happen to undermine your efforts:

Timeliness - or lack thereof. An event or topic which would have been highly relevant and appropriate has already peaked and to start preparing content now would result in arriving in the conversation late, not making the best use of the opportunity.

Resource issues - whilst you have identified a current event which is gaining traction, your team may not be available to produce the content.

Approval - you have no issues with the above, but you can't get the appropriate person internally to approve the content in time.

Quality - you successfully publish the content, but ultimately, it doesn't resonate with the intended audience and performs poorly.

To address these, you need a clear process for reactive content:

Identify your moment

With millions of things happening worldwide every day, how do we know which ones are appropriate to bring into your social media?

You may want to focus on content which is fast growing in popularity but is still in the early stages of its lifecycle, hence it is yet to peak. Tools such as Buzzsumo, YouTube's 'Trending' chart, Twitter / X's 'trends' list and Google Trends will offer some valuable insights for this. On top of the mentioned tools, simply being active as a consumer on social media will help you stay alert to topics and trends.

Whilst several key trends will be apparent at any one time, you should have a guide to what kind of things your club will engage with, and more importantly, what kind of events you want to avoid.

It is likely that you will want to engage, where relevant, with universal news events such as Sporting Events, the World Cup or widely admired footballing personalities passing.

Brief Creative

Once you've ideated and developed your idea into a defined piece of content, brief your creative producers. Again, this all may be a single person.

You will need to include in the document:

- **Image or video** - be clear about dimensions and technical specs. If a video, a basic hand-drawn storyboard or detailed script will help speed up production and subsequent amends.
- **Copy** - be clear about limits but offer creative freedom
- **Hashtags** - research which passion areas this plays into if any. Be aware of using too many [or any at all] as reactive content must not look or feel like marketing.
- **Platform** - specific requirements - any particular specifications for all channels you intend to publish on.
- **Deadlines** - be clear about your timeliness needs and allow contingency for amends and approval.

Production

As content is produced, continue to monitor the conversation as it plays out on social media. Keep in communication with your content producers to ensure the content remains relevant when it is published.

Approval

You will need to agree with the people at the club who will approve you, or your team's, content.

- **If you have full autonomy of the marketing output -**
    - If you're leading a team, then you should be the final point of approval for any content.
    - If you have created the content yourself, you should always have someone to sense check your own content. Not so much as an approval, but more so to check for any errors.

- **If you do not have full autonomy of the marketing output -**
    - Agree on who should have the final sign off of any content
    - You should check over all content before it is sent to be signed off

There are several check-ins you should perform to receive approval for your content idea.

The first one would be when the opportunity first presents itself and you're planning to create some reactive content. At this stage, your point of approval may give the green [or red!] light to the very idea of associating your club with a particular event.

Next, when you form a brief, you should again seek outline approval to ensure stakeholders are aware of the creative route.

Finally, once the content has been produced, the person/team appointed should feel involved, well-informed, and in a good place to approve the completed piece.

As this process likely relies on asynchronous communication such as email, timelines can easily become drawn out. The recommendation is to always speak directly with your point of contact via phone, in person or through another platform such as Slack or Skype. You will find that over time, the process becomes quicker and easier as all people involved become accustomed to the requirements of the process and the importance of speedy timeliness.

Publish

Once approved, the final step in getting your reactive content live is publishing it on the social media platforms which you previously identified as appropriate for leveraging the opportunity.

This is your final chance to ensure all your media and copy is error-free and still relevant for the conversation as it stands at this second.

Example

At Stenhousemuir, we recently ran a tongue-in-cheek joke about Barcelona's limited edition Rolling Stones shirt.

The first four steps below all took place within an hour, as it's vitally important to hit these opportunities as early as possible. If the CMO delayed in agreeing to run with the post, it would have affected the reach, engagement and overall success of the post.

FC Barcelona @FCBarcelona · Oct 19

Paint it, Blaugrana 👕💙❤️

FC Barcelona 🤝 @rollingstones 🤝 @spotify

💬 271 🔁 2K ❤️ 17K 📊 2.5M 🔖 ⬆️

Stenhousemuir FC @StenhousemuirFC · Oct 19

As part of our agreement with **Loc Hire**, Saturday's kit against Peterhead will feature the popular "Portable Toilet", available to **hire** today from **Loc Hire**

#WeAreWarriors ⚔️

FC Barcelona @FCBarcelona · Oct 19

Paint it, Blaugrana 👕💙❤️

FC Barcelona 🟡 @rollingstones 🟡 @spotify

💬 18 🔁 191 ❤️ 1.2K 📊 539K 🔖 ⬆️

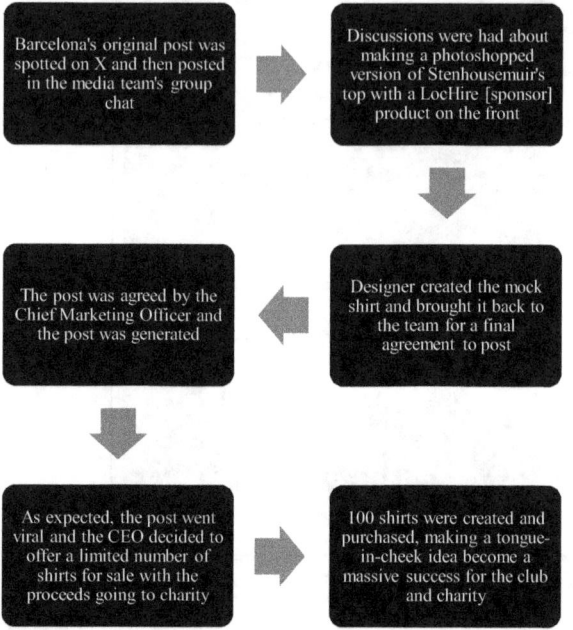

However, some posts may need a longer approval process, which is why it's important to have your plans in place.

Monitor

Pressing "Send" or "Publish" for your content is not the end of the process!

As you have entered an active conversation, you are likely to receive a multitude of responses to your post from all sides of the discussion. Be ready to respond accordingly, thanking for praise but not over-explaining your motives to detractors.

In situations where the creative backfires, does not land in the way you'd hoped, or you cannot fully stand behind the content [perhaps in cases of basic misjudgement], you need to be prepared to delete your content.

Tips for implementing your content plan

The focus of this section is to introduce you to the topic of collaboration, highlighting the best practices to support you in the creation of your content plan.

Collaboration

A successful plan is easier to implement and manage if all relevant people can access it. And the easiest way to do that is to make it accessible online.

You can upload the content planner template [http://bit.ly/37jKGId] to Google Drive, or recreate them in a shared task management system such as Trello or CoSchedule. You can find these systems, online at https://trello.com or https://coschedule.com

No matter which option you choose, you should be aware that different collaborators will need different levels of access rights. Give Read-Only access to anyone who may want to provide input into, or see updates from, the social media platforms. Reserving Write access only for the person or team who act specifically as Social Media Editor.

Publish content according to what is in the plan, and when you leverage topical opportunities at short notice, be sure to record these, marking them with a specific tag or colour.

Your content calendar will serve as an archive of what happened [or didn't happen, and why] each day. This way, you'll be able to review at a glance what your balance of content was across channels, formats, curated vs created, planned vs reactive.

Curation vs creation

You can plan your original content months in advance.

Your content calendar, on the other hand, can only contain placeholder entries for the curation of content from other sources, as this will largely be re-shared shortly after it is published.

To develop successful curation on your social media channels it is important to follow the most relevant and high-quality accounts in your niche or industry. This will give you lots of fresh content to cherry pick for curation on your own channels.

Curation best practice

Copyright is not usually a problem when it comes to social media. Technically, your profiles don't belong to your club. They are the property of the social media platforms themselves.

Nonetheless, there are a few reasons why it is worth respecting the best practice when posting content which does not belong to you.

These best practices mainly revolve around the concept of growing and maintaining the reputation of respectful users of the platforms. On top of this, you need to use curation as an opportunity to connect with the creator of the content – by mentioning them or tagging their account in your post.

Show that you credit good content when you find and share it and think about ways to start a discussion around curated content that brings in its creator from the start. Social media is a community, and you need to use its nature to your advantage, by fostering a sense of reciprocal generosity in your curated output.

Remember...

- **Creation**
  - o Any original content created by your club
- **Curation**
  - o Any content not created by your club, but posted on your club's channels
    - ▪ Vlogger videos, sponsorship videos etc.

Scheduling

Whether original or curated, it's usually most efficient to schedule your content to ensure that posts go out exactly when planned - whether or not your final line of approval is available.

Take into consideration other factors which determine who you are reaching, when and how.

Schedule your social media activity accordingly. You can use a variety of tools to support you. These include:

Buffer

When scheduling your Facebook, Instagram, Twitter/X, LinkedIn and Pinterest activities, you can manage a large number of accounts through Buffer.

This tool will let you schedule and queue future social updates across a variety of platforms, focusing on simplicity and ease of use. If you install the browser extension, you can share content found on the web through your social accounts in a matter of seconds, as well as being able to craft your own original posts using the tool's dashboard.

The basic premise is that while you can schedule for specific times, you can now also keep adding content to your queue, and it will go out at regular pre-set intervals. Such tools are great for content-heavy clubs who can fill up the content queue in the morning, and see their posts go out throughout the day.

Buffer can be found at this link https://buffer.com.

There is a free option to plan and schedule your content across three channels, with paid options available for more users and channels to be covered. For all of your team to have access to the three main social media channels [Facebook, Instagram and X] will cost $36 per month.

Hootsuite

Offering more complex functionality than Buffer, Hootsuite acts more like a social content calendar dashboard. It connects to a higher number of social media platforms and has a wealth of features for enterprises. The platform allows team collaboration and provides analytics. It can also facilitate paid promotion of your content thanks to its boost tool.

Hootsuite can be found at this link https://www.hootsuite.com

Due to the complex functions, Hootsuite is an expensive option and will cost £89 per month for a single user with access to 10 channels.

Publer

Similar to Buffer, Publer allows you to plan and schedule your content across the main social media channels.

Publer lets you schedule and queue future social updates across a variety of platforms, focusing on simplicity and ease of use.

The basic premise is that while you can schedule for specific times, you can now also keep adding content to your queue, and it will go out at regular pre-set intervals. Such tools are great for content-heavy clubs who can fill up the content queue in the morning, and see their posts go out throughout the day.

You can find Publer at this link https://publer.io/

A single user with access to 3 social media accounts will cost £9.49 per month. If you wish to add in a full analytics suite for your 3 channels, it will cost £16.61.

These are just a few examples of Social Media scheduling systems and there are loads more out there. If you do want to invest here, it's important that you shop around for the best deals for what is most relevant to your club. Some also offer discounts for charities, so check to see if your club can qualify.

Long Term – Mastering Football Marketing

Developing a social media strategy

In this section, you will develop your understanding of social strategies and find out how to implement omni-channel and multi-channel strategic planning.

Why do you need a social media strategy?

Did you know that the average person in the UK sees between 158 and 838 adverts per day. So, while getting your club noticed is important, reinforcing your message is the key to gaining a response.

Successful social media relies on a fully integrated, strategic approach. While quick, tactical, activity can seem fruitful and satisfying in the short term, you can't build your club's brand without managing your entire communications output.

If done right, supporters will see each of your communications platforms as one cohesive entity- whether they are buying a programme at a match or responding to one of your tweets.

To get into this mindset, keep asking yourself questions like:

- How could a kit launch stimulate online traffic?
- Why would people share my upcoming social post?

Thinking strategically in this way, rather than treating social media as an afterthought, is vital to success in the channel.

Your strategy should guide an effective approach

A well-defined social media strategy will detail exactly how your club conducts itself across social media, and what content it publishes.

Make sure you keep this strategy broad, describing processes and guidelines around things like tone of voice, who your audience is and if you have any locally competitive clubs. Avoid being too specific about the exact channels and tools that you use, as these are ever-changing and likely to render your strategy obsolete before long.

Use club goals and audience insight to determine social channels

Your choice of social media platform should be dictated by your wider marketing aims. Whilst the temptation might be to have as many social accounts as possible, this stretches resources and may result in a lack of focus and clarity.

Think about the wider needs of your club and its marketing. How could the key social channels drive these, and which ones are relevant for your club?

Cross-channel content

For a genuinely multi-channel or omni-channel experience, you'll need a planning process that works across your whole club. Without this, you run the risk of concepts, activities and content being planned in siloed channels.

This creates a disjointed experience for the supporter, resulting in a reduced impact and, ultimately, a reduced revenue from the activity. Consider how you can keep your entire marketing mix integrated, and cross-promote to supporters of your various formats.

The easiest way to do this is to re-purpose the same content across several channels.

For example, if a player wins a player of the month award, you may use the same graphics across your channels, but for LinkedIn you may edit your copy to focus on the players, or award sponsors, while still celebrating your player's win.

Facilitating a collaborative process

If your club allows, you will be working with several people. Seamless collaboration is crucial to the success of your strategy.

Whether working across internal teams or with supporters and sponsors, there are many challenges to overcome. This is best done by having a well-defined strategy.

Communication

Team communication can be difficult to neatly coordinate and is one of the main causes of mistakes or delays in projects. Luckily, communication solutions have evolved in recent years.

Email remains the default business channel but can be unwieldy for large group conversations and isn't helpful for newcomers who start with an empty inbox. An alternative is using instant messaging platforms like WhatsApp and Messenger. However, asking individuals to install apps on their own devices can blur the line between work and personal spaces, which is not healthy for employees.

Slack offers a best-of-both-worlds. Sitting between instant messaging and email, it has exploded in popularity.

It offers cross-device direct and group message functionality much like WhatsApp, meaning that conversations and files can be shared within teams. Additionally, because all 'channels' are constant and remain as a record of each team, anyone new can catch up with previous discussions.

Consider creating a Slack workspace for your next campaign or project. Inviting people to relevant channels keeps all conversations in one place, whilst facilitating group video calls, file-sharing, and integrations with other marketing software.

Slack is available at this link https://slack.com/intl/en-gb/ and prices start at £5.75 per person, per month.

There are other communication platforms also available such as Microsoft Teams and Monday.com

You can also set up a Discord server which is a free service and offers many of the options that you would pay for on the services above.

Asset Management

Fortunately, the days of files being stuck on offline computers or servers are behind us, with file sharing and collaboration becoming commonplace.

Two services – Dropbox and Google Drive – have driven this change offering two similar solutions.

Dropbox

Dropbox keeps a team's files synchronised across any number of devices, allowing these files to be sent to external recipients with a web link. This ensures that assets, sometimes large in file size, such as photos and video are accessible for everyone at all times.

URL	https://www.dropbox.com
Monthly price	Benefits
£7.99	1 user / 2TB / Up to 2GB file size
£18	2 user / 3TB / Up to 100GB file size
£16 per user	3+ users / 9TB / Up to 100GB file size
£20 per user	3+ users / 15TB / Up to 250GB file size

Google Drive

While Google Drive offers the file sharing capability of Dropbox it is not as user-friendly or universally effective. However, the service excels in real-time document collaboration, allowing multiple users to edit the same text document, spreadsheet or presentation at the same time.

This becomes particularly useful where different stakeholders need to input. Examples include social media content calendars, budget plans and KPI reports where metrics from many different sources are pulled together.

URL	https://drive.google.com
Monthly price	Benefits
Free	15GB
£1.59	100GB
£2.49	200GB
£7.99	2TB

Approval and publishing workflow

There are several models for structuring social media teams and lines of approval. One of the most common mirrors digital publishing, placing an editor at the centre of a team of contributors as the gatekeeper of social content.

In larger teams, multiple people can be appointed to the role of social media editor, one for each platform. However, in most instances, a single person is sufficient. For smaller clubs, it may only be one person across all channels.

For clubs with a social media team, only the 'editor' should have administrator rights on the content calendar and their role is to dictate the exact content that is published. Copy images and videos can be approved only by the editor, while community managers might then do the actual posting. Like in other media, the editor commissions content from specialists in the team as well as accepting proposals for pieces of content. Either way, ultimately, the editor is responsible for defining [and refining] the content's format and form. For smaller clubs, this whole process may be completed by a single person.

Executing a strategy without creating reams of unnecessary conversations can be a challenge. The aim should be to centralise a "single source of truth", i.e. one place for everyone in the team to go and find what is happening or has happened, when, and by whom. Google Drive is one of the most effective solutions to achieve this.

Alternatives include Asana and Trello. These project management tools offer a high level of flexibility, making them suitable for a variety of processes. Projects can be planned, updated, and each task can be assigned to a specific person within the platform.

Successful social media teams implement these tools into a well-structured process which all staff or volunteers are required to follow.

Example

At Stenhousemuir FC, we have a media team WhatsApp group where we can plan and organise as well as share what we've seen and liked.

For data storage, we use Google Drive and all members have access. In the Drive, we have set up clear folders to ensure that everything is easy to find.

Here is how our Drive looks.

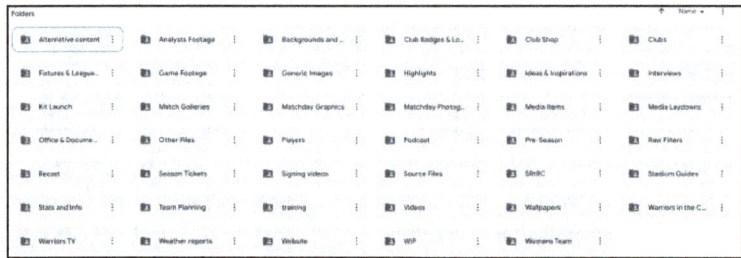

Inside the Fixtures folder, it is further broken down by competition.

Going deeper, inside the League Two folder, all the fixtures are listed.

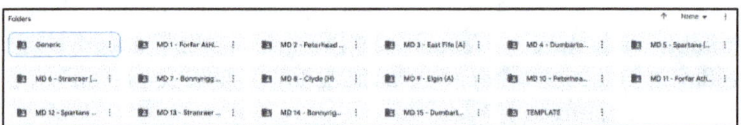

Each fixture folder is broken into three sections with all the relevant graphics and documents in those folders. This makes it easy for any member of the team to post and schedule content.

Tone of voice

Key to a winning social media strategy is the definition and implementation of a consistent club tone.

Remember that a club's [or any brand] social media-specific tone is likely to be different from the core tone of voice as it represents the more conversational, human, side of the club.

When collaborating with others it is important to ensure that they are aware of the social media style guide.

This should define:

- How we write with 'do and don't' examples
- What images we use and how we edit them, with examples
- How we use our own club branding, with 'do and don't' examples
- How we interact with supporters, sponsors and other clubs and fans
- How/if we deal with contentious topics
- How we deal with praise and complaints
- How each member of staff interacts with the club on social media

Developing a social media channel strategy

In this section, you will start to apply what you understand about objectives and audiences, bringing them into your overarching social media strategy.

What your social media strategy should include

A social media channel strategy should take a holistic view across your social media channels.

It should articulate:

- **Who** your audience is,
- **Which** channels to use to target them
- **What** content resonates with them.

It will also set out what your objectives for social are for the year, allowing you to measure progress from month to month. This will equip you to consider response times, followers, and sentiment across the year. The supporter experience of your club will suffer if you only focus your efforts on key campaigns.

Platform Planning

There are too many channels for you to use them all effectively, so you must choose the ones that will deliver the most value for your club and your supporters. The chart below shows the features and tools of the nine core social channels.

The chart below gives you an easy visualisation of each of the core social media platforms and their features/tools.

	Facebook	Twitter	Instagram	Pinterest	Tik Tok	Snapchat	YouTube	Linkedin	WhatsApp
Search Optimised	✓	✓	✓	✓			✓		
Customer Service	✓	✓				✓			✓
Live Video	✓	✓	✓		✓	✓	✓	✓	
Real-time Conversation		✓			✓	✓			✓
Long-term Content	✓		✓				✓	✓	
Lead Generation	✓	✓	✓	✓				✓	
Visual Brand Storytelling	✓		✓	✓	✓	✓	✓		
Authority Building	✓	✓					✓	✓	✓
Talent Acquisition	✓	✓						✓	
Great for Influencers			✓		✓		✓		
Social Commerce	✓		✓	✓	✓	✓			

It can be easy to fall into the trap of thinking that you need to be on as many social media platforms as possible. This will encourage you to focus on low-impact generic content which can be repurposed into different formats. Instead, pick the few channels that best match your requirements and concentrate on filling those channels with the best possible content.

In other words; do less, better.

Your choice here will not only improve your marketing results but can also say something about your club.

Targeting the right audience

Another essential factor to consider when defining your channel strategy is the demographic makeup of users for each channel.

Channel	Monthly Users*	Male	Female
Facebook	40 million	48%	52%
Instagram	24 million	46%	54%
X [Twitter]	13.6 million	60%	40%
Snapchat	17.5 million	44%	56%
LinkedIn	27 million	60%	40%

*LinkedIn figure is registered users

However, while this information is good to know, it does not mean that you should go to extremes and put 'Male' content on Twitter/X, and 'Female' content on Snapchat.

Objective Setting for Social Media Channels

Setting KPIs can be difficult, as metrics vary greatly between the different social media channels. Also, be aware that engagement levels are also industry dependent. Therefore, the best way to start is by benchmarking against clubs that match your level or aspirational level.

Use tools such as *FanpageKarma* and *Followerwonk* to find and compare similar profiles to your own.
There are two types of benchmarking to take into consideration: your aspirational benchmarks and your direct competitors' benchmarks.

You can find *FanpageKarma* at this link https://www.fanpagekarma.com.

Although *FanpageKarma* is a useful tool, it is very expensive with prices starting at $69 per month for a single channel of your choice.

Followerwonk is a cheaper alternative and can be found at this link https://followerwonk.com. There's lots of tools that you can use for free.

Aspirational benchmark

Which other club is performing at the level you'd like your content to achieve? The one whose results are realistically achievable by your club within a defined timeframe.

Direct competitors' benchmark

Who are you currently similar to? What results are they achieving?

The answer to these questions will highlight any urgent issues. Perhaps, your club has a similar size to one of the competitors, and whilst they lead you slightly in supporters or followers, you have a drastically lower engagement rate on posts. This tells you that your content needs to become more engaging before you attempt to compete with your aspirational benchmark.

Benchmarks allow you to understand what "good" looks like on each channel for your sport, comparing it with your position. Once you have completed your benchmarking activity, you can start to work on your Social Media Channel Strategy.

Documenting a Social Media Channel Strategy

This section will look at creating your social media strategy. You can download a template at http://bit.ly/2NuV7S9. This section will guide you through the creation of your own strategy document.

Club Goals

The key club goals, from which marketing and social media objectives are derived. Keeping these at the top of the strategy document ensures you remain aligned to these throughout your efforts on social media.

Marketing objectives

These detail how the marketing department is contributing to the club goals and will refer directly to driving awareness, consideration, conversion and loyalty through communications-led activity.

Social media objectives

Create SMART objectives for your strategy based on the marketing objectives. Create any number of them, as required by your overarching marketing goals, and ensure they are specific to each platform.

Audience

Define the core supporter groups and audiences you will target with this strategy. If you're lucky, you may have two main sources of this information - from your social media platform insights, and from existing club personas, if your club has this documented.

Compare the two, do they match? There may be a particular demographic skew in your social audience, and this is important to take into account.

Beware of your social insights pushing you towards very broad audiences [e.g. men in the UK aged 18-35]. This can damage your marketing, making it so general that it fails to resonate with anyone in particular.

As the old saying goes, *"if you're marketing to everyone, you're marketing to no-one"*. Find more specific information out about your typical followers in social and look at individual profiles to help characterise them. If they differ from your club personas, create new personas for social media.

Channels

Refer to the link at the start of this section, based on your goals, objectives and target audiences, decide which channels meet your needs.

Detail each channel's role and objectives. Make sure you include, for each:

- **How** will your club leverage the functionality, the culture, the reach of this platform?
- **What** aspects of your club's personality will come out strongest on this particular social platform?
- **Which** subset of your supporters could you reach here?

Overall, it should be clear what the key opportunities that operating on each platform presents to your club.

Developing a social media campaign strategy

In this section, you will learn the Help, Hub and Hero framework to plan your content on social media.

Developing a social media campaign strategy

When it comes to digital marketing, traditional channels such as advertising or direct mail have to adapt to the new environment.

Unlike other channels, which are merely presented to an audience, digital marketing focuses on driving actions, be it a click-through or an email sign-up. This need to drive action will dictate the content you produce.

Because social media channels are constantly 'on', the audience can access them whenever they want. For this reason, it is critical for social media channels to always have up to date content to respond to an audience's every need.

To be successful, a social media strategy must plan two types of communication:

Ongoing communications: which give consistency to the channel.

Campaign-specific communications: which run during a specified period.

Most of the larger clubs will have a plan of key campaigns throughout the year, in particular things like,

- Season ticket sales
- Kit launches
- Player of the Year awards

These are separate from planning your channel strategy, as they will have their own objectives and budgets, but should still

109

support or contribute to the channel objectives and channel success.

Social media campaigns provide bursts of reach and engagement over and above the day-to-day posts and responses. To explain this tiered approach to publishing in social media, Google popularised the 'help, hub, hero' framework for content planning.

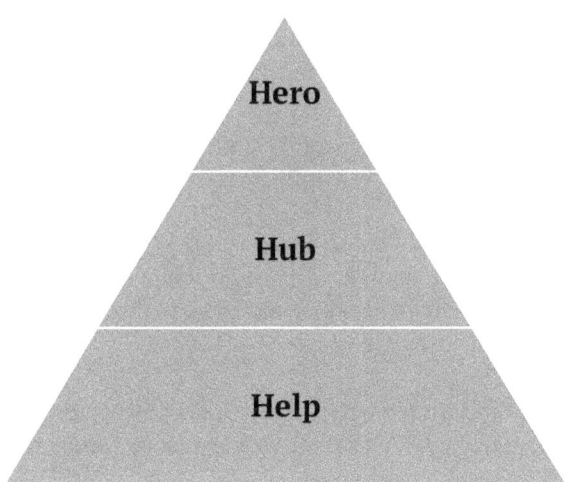

Hero

Those big tent-pole moments in the year that generate high levels of awareness among a much broader audience. These will usually be kit launches and season ticket sales.

Hub

You publish **Hub** content which is tied to new signings and behind the scenes information, providing a fresh perspective of your club.

Help

You provide always-on content for your most engaged and loyal audience with **Help** content. This will mainly be matchday content, weekly news bulletins etc. This falls into your channel strategy, while the following **Hub** and **Hero** approaches would fall into individual campaign strategies.

Usually, social media campaigns are tied to Hub and Hero content. They are a fundamental part of your yearly plan as they give you spikes of activity that go beyond the day-to-day posting, generating waves of interest and pushing the current wider club's goals.

Why you need a campaign strategy

Creating a campaign-specific strategy is a vital first step in deploying a social media campaign. This should take the form of a document made accessible to all key stakeholders through a collaboration tool such as Google Drive or Dropbox.

The purpose is to make sure the campaign is focused on pushing the social media channel goals as set out in your 'social media channel strategy'.

Many social campaigns can be heavily idea-led, so the temptation could be to execute an interesting idea or exploit a new social platform functionality. But you have to make sure that you maintain your focus on your set objectives.

Creating your campaign strategy

Club Goal

What are the club's goals for this campaign?

Campaign Objectives

What are the objectives of this activity?

Remember to use the SMART objective setting framework to ensure your objectives are valuable and useful. These objectives can relate to any aspect of the campaign and any channel that it might affect.

Remember, SMART stands for **S**pecific, **M**easurable, **A**ttainable, **R**ealistic and **T**imely.

Social media objectives

Define the social objectives that this piece of activity will contribute to achieving.

Audience

Who is the audience for this specific campaign? While you have already defined the audience targeted with your social media platform/s, a campaign may have a more specific, or even broader, target audience. Usually, it is likely to be the former, as social media is particularly well suited for highly targeted campaigns. The majority of your campaigns will be aimed at supporters, but there may be other opportunities that go beyond your own supporter base. Think about attracting local businesses and sponsors and how you would target them.

Remember to describe your audience beyond simple demographic terms. It is important to mention their likely age, gender and location. However, to really tailor your campaign creatively, you will need to find out more about your audience:

- Interests
- Attitudes
- Other clubs or accounts they consume and engage with
- When and how they like to consume content
- Their information needs - if relevant
- Who they see as an authority or influencer for your type of content

Channels

A social media campaign does not necessarily have to live within all your chosen social media channels. Depending on the campaign objectives and targeted audience, you may want to only use some of these channels. You may even decide to use a platform which is not part of the core brand channel strategy, such as Snapchat or YouTube, to trial a temporary campaign on.

Pick the channel/s you want to use for the campaign and specify how you plan to use them. Explain why each one will effectively carry your campaign message to the target audience and contribute to your campaign objectives.

Social Media Content Strategy

In this section, you will learn the benefits of using a broad spectrum of content formats from audio to video to written and interactive content.

Mapping Your Content

Once you've planned your content, you need to decide on the way that you will articulate your findings. Different topics, at different stages in the customer journey, will lend themselves to certain media formats.

For example, videos and articles or blogs are great for information-seekers who will come across your club in their research. This is known as 'inbound marketing' whereby prospects get to you as part of an active search for information [as opposed to being interrupted by an advert].

Alternatively, viral content like quizzes and competitions are great at reaching beyond the edges of your existing network.

It's important to have a good spread of content to ensure your content is moving people along your customer journey. Whether it's making new visitors aware of your club, reactivating long-term supporters, or everyone in between.

Video Content

The importance of video content is hard to overstate, yet it remains underused by many marketers.

Video is the best performing content type on Facebook, and, according to *Sprout Social*, LinkedIn users are 20 times more likely to share a video on the platform than any other type of post*.

Think about how your ideas and existing content could be turned into videos. If you don't have that skill set in your team, you may be missing out on a huge opportunity.

Additionally, consider that YouTube is the second-largest search engine after Google and one of the world's most popular repositories of knowledge. Imagine how your club content could be relayed visually. How could you show, rather than tell, club information and deliver this informational value in a format they prefer to consume?

A great example of making video content work for you was this video by Plymouth Argyle which has been viewed over 11,000 times in the last year.
https://www.youtube.com/watch?v=TXQHFEknEDE

- Source: https://sproutsocial.com/insights/linkedin-statistics/

Written Content

In a world of interactive, immersive, moving content, the written word has retained its age-old place as the key source of high-value information.

Text-based content, of any form, is a vital asset for your club. It is something you accumulate, growing in value for your supporters and yourself.

Let's look at the key reasons why text provides so many opportunities for clubs:

- Today, search engines still favour text - it's easier to analyse and categorise. Your text content offers detailed information to a search engine's algorithm about who your club is.
- Text can be instantly translated into any language, so caters for a global audience.
- It remains the most manageable and, ultimately, valuable way to store authoritative information.

116

- Even as the volume of your content grows into large quantities, it remains easy to point someone to a specific article or even sentence through referencing and hyperlinking.
- It can be read out by screen readers or virtual assistants such as Siri and Alexa, providing maximum accessibility to users with special needs.
- Accessing text requires the most basic technology - both device and network-side, meaning this content is accessible for anyone online.

For the majority of clubs, written content primarily takes the form of articles and blogs. The news articles published on your club's website should be seen as the core of your whole content marketing operation. It is, quite literally, the source text of your club - the most undiluted account of your ethos, your people, your club and your knowledge.

It is also the home of your content. Videos, Instagram feeds and posts on X, can all be embedded here so that your website can be the most comprehensive content experience for a supporter.

Whether you turn it into audio podcasts, caption videos, tweets or guest blogs on other websites, your written content can be endlessly repurposed and reinterpreted in different formats.

Visual Content

As humans, we are visual creatures. We pay attention to and remember visual information better than any other type of information.

Images support the understanding of concepts, it's the way humans learn and comprehend. Some studies show how people following instructions with text and illustrations perform 323% better than people who learn without illustrations.

TOP TIP:

> **In social media, images are crucial. Posts with images receive 150% more reposts than tweets without images. Facebook posts with images see 2.3 x more engagement than those without.**

Whilst stock libraries can provide high-quality imagery to help make your point in social media [with Unsplash remaining one of the strongest - https://unsplash.com] you should look to invest in creating your own original imagery that stands out in fast-moving social feeds.

In fact, visual information also helps us to remember text or audio information. For instance, it has been observed that when a person hears and understands a piece of information, only three days later, they will remember just 10% of it. Add a picture to the audio and they will remember 65%.

Facebook

Facebook users are typically looking for emotional or entertaining content. Share incredible, inspirational or surprising photography. Think about personal stories and moments captured visually. Bring humour with memes and highly relatable or topical content.

Instagram

People open their Instagram app to see beautiful things, places and lifestyle. Think of it like a magazine full of aspirational objects that people covet, incredible places they want to go, and amazing experiences they would like to partake in.

How could you articulate your club's purpose and message via beautiful photography?

X [Twitter]

X's use in the world is mainly around news and information. People use the platform to get real-time updates on events happening in a particular moment in time. Users go on X to also keep abreast of an industry or niche they are interested in. Humour is also very important on X.

The imagery on the platform works best when it is highly informative, such as small infographics, charts and graphs. These can be supported by commentary in the tweet, or indeed a thread of multiple posts explaining and discussing your key points.

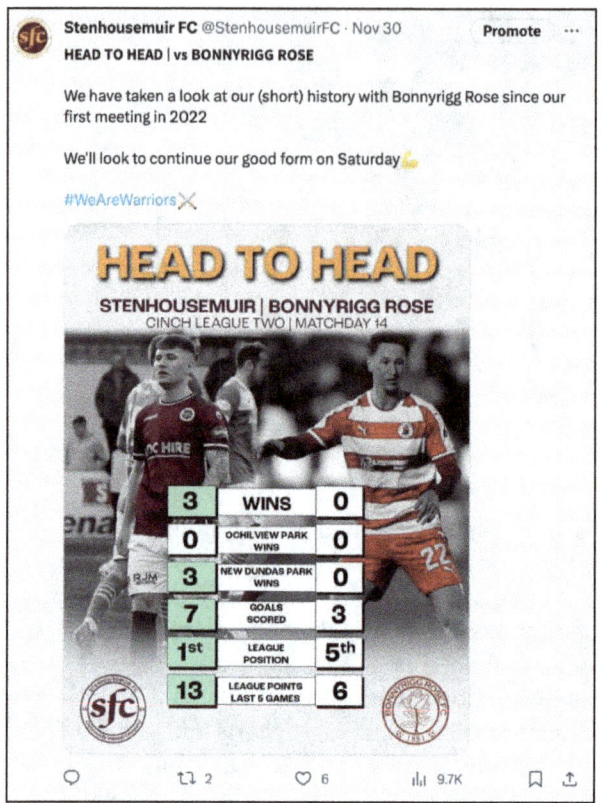

Pinterest

People use Pinterest like a search engine- primarily for things, not people. What objects and places make up your club? Could you place them in the Pinterest ecosystem? Bear in mind that all images can link to an external website so there are potential traffic benefits.

LinkedIn

The power of images has become apparent on LinkedIn in recent years. Most updates in the feed are now accompanied by an image, with the platform also introducing videos.

How can you take the corporate side of your club and visualise it for an audience of potential sponsors, partners and staff?

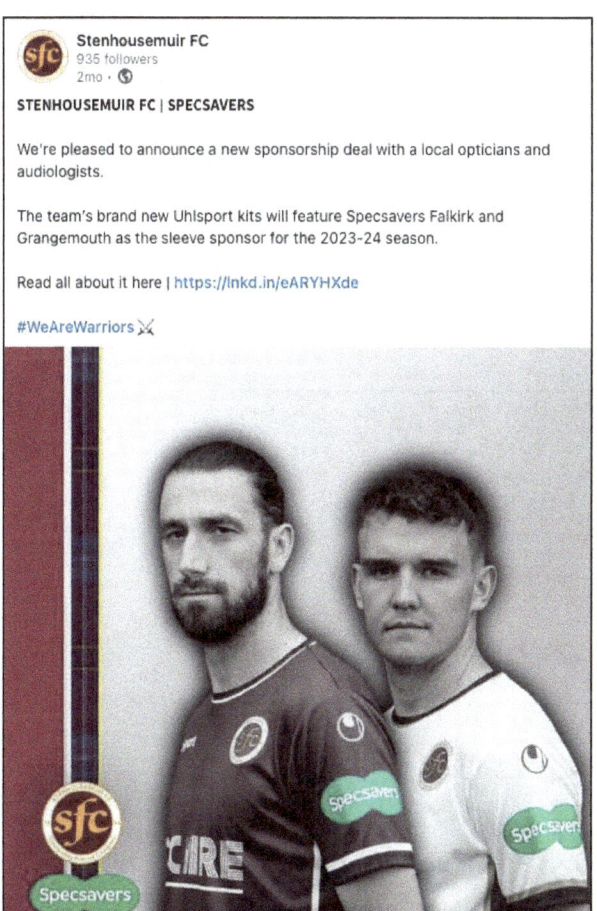

Interactive Content

Whilst requiring higher investment in terms of user time and effort, interactive content creates a much more valuable engagement with your supporters, developing a deep and lasting relationship between them and your club.

This can take the form of relatively casual interactions such as fun polls and quizzes. These can be ways to test the supporter's appetite for something more complex. These are also a highly effective means of gathering audience insight unavailable elsewhere. Social media insights tools can tell you plenty about the basic demographics of your audience, but to find out what they think about your club and competitors, you need to use polls and surveys.

Consider questions that are fun and easy to answer while also giving you some valuable data. Use polling tools on each social network to ask different questions to different sections of your audience.

Stenhousemuir FC @StenhousemuirFC · Dec 2
Who's Playlist is it Anyhow ?!

Edin Lynch	19.2%
Zak McKay	25%
Kinlay Bilham	25%
Mikey Anderson	30.8%

52 votes · Final results

◯ 1   ⇄   ♡ 1   ılı 2.9K   🔖 ⬆

Stenhousemuir FC @StenhousemuirFC · Dec 2
Believe it or not, our DJ this week was Edin!

◯   ⇄   ♡ 3   ılı 1.7K   🔖 ⬆

Audio Content

Audio-only content has grown in popularity since the advent of podcasts in the early 2000s. The format has gained traction due to the breadth of content available on a vast number of topics. It is estimated there are currently 700,000 podcast shows consisting of 29 million episodes.

Podcast listeners tend to be affluent, educated and tech-savvy. The traditional male skew of the format is diminishing as time goes on, with the male majority among listeners standing at just 56% in 2019.

Clubs have been slow to include this format as part of their content marketing, approaching it cautiously due to the intimidatingly high-quality standard of popular podcasts being intimidatingly high. Nonetheless, some clubs have found success by keeping the formats simple with good quality and informative content. Podcasts allow clubs to discuss in-depth their core news items, bringing key people to life and allowing the supporters to hear their voice and their stories with authenticity.

There are some good podcasts to draw inspiration from. The Clyde FC and Peterhead FC Podcasts are good to listen to, or the Sports Marketing Scotland podcast is also extremely useful, not so much for learning how to run your own podcast, but it also covers lots of topics that will be of use to football marketers.

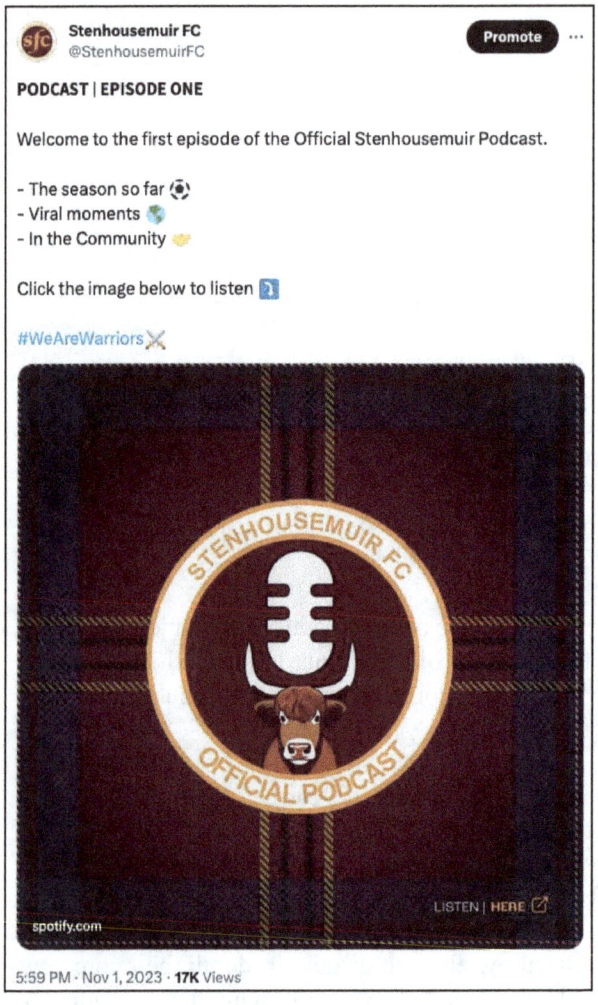

Stenhousemuir FC
@StenhousemuirFC

Promote ...

PODCAST | EPISODE ONE

Welcome to the first episode of the Official Stenhousemuir Podcast.

- The season so far ⚽
- Viral moments 🌍
- In the Community 🤝

Click the image below to listen 🔈

#WeAreWarriors ⚔️

LISTEN | HERE ↗

spotify.com

5:59 PM · Nov 1, 2023 · **17K** Views

Social Media Fan Experience

Learn how to pull together guidelines on how your club should approach fans on your social media feeds. Although you will mainly interact with your own supporters, this is still considered as customer service.

Responding to supporters and other fans

People are talking about your club night and day, whether you like it or not. How are you going to respond to this?

In most instances, you can benefit from joining those conversations, either to address negative comments or to further positive discussions.

Through ongoing social monitoring, you should have access to these conversations, and have an efficient system of alerts. A simple email or integration with a corporate messaging service such as Slack, that alerts the appropriate staff will ensure you step in promptly.

Additionally, you should formulate a basic guide to how your club responds to certain categories of complaint, and to what extent it joins in with casual conversations.

For the majority of complaints [complaints about food, live stream issues, stadium access etc. you can usually direct them to a club official email account].

Customer [supporters and non-supporters] service as marketing

The overall objective with this activity is to repeatedly show the world what kind of club you are, and what kind of people work within the club.

The rise of social media and club transparency has lifted the veil on how clubs are run. Because of this, the general public now demands far more in terms of ethics and ethos from clubs.

Interacting with your supporters and prospects in social media plays perfectly into this modern development, allowing you to display the human side of your club. Certainly, it requires all staff or volunteers to be trained and briefed accordingly, communicating the club's values consistently over time. And, critically, never out of step.

Introduction

A brief to social media managers involved in this work needs to include:

Brief, Step 1

General guidelines on how the club sounds on social media. This is not necessarily the same as the wider club tone and is probably more conversational.

Brief, Step 2

Clarity on the kind of words the club uses to communicate. Do we say "great" or "cool"? "Thanks" or "Cheers"?

Brief, Step 3

What's the structure of a complaint response? For experienced clubs [and other businesses], this tends to be:

- Friendly, personal greeting – "Hi John"
- Full and sincere apology, with genuine empathy – "We're so sorry to hear about your issue buying tickets and how frustrating it's been".
- Commitment to resolve, with realistic expectations – "We'll get this sorted for you as soon as we can".

- Personal staff sign-off – "Thanks, Ian"

Brief, Step 4

A convenient and memorable way to communicate your parameters for social interactions, a concise list of practical examples will demonstrate to staff and volunteers exactly how to respond to supporters online. There won't be too many complaints to deal with, so you could build a response repository to the main type of fan complaints.

Brief, Step 5

Take a variety of real situations and show how they were dealt with. Be sure to clarify the need for all responses to be personal and bespoke, to some extent. Canned, generic, responses straight from the playbook can frustrate and annoy supporters.

Customer service at scale

Manual, one-to-one, communication can become labour intensive. But there are several ways to effectively engage supporters on a large scale.

Scripted or 'canned' responses are an essential part of the online customer service toolkit. But you must make sure that these responses look sufficiently personalised to be received as genuine. Online fans do share complaint responses and may feel worse if you give them the same apology script as everyone else.

Additionally, on a growing number of social platforms, you can set up chatbots to handle the initial phase of a customer conversation. On Facebook's Messenger platform, these chatbots can provide complex functionality, can greet supporters, and even hold complete conversations.

Routing serious complaints

While most negative feedback on social media will consist of minor grievances with a club, there may be occasions where you will have to deal with more serious issues. As a football club, you will always attract negative feedback from supporters, non-supporters, and internet trolls.

Where you may feel passionate and protective of your club, it's important that you do not interact with any trolls. They only want to elicit a response from the club, and you will enter a no-win situation if you acknowledge them in public.

An example of this might be an abusive former member of staff or volunteer who feels like an issue has not been resolved and has made it their mission to get your online attention – no matter whether it is positive or negative. Not only is social media not the best channel of communication for resolution, but it's crucial to get this potentially damaging discussion off a public platform to be dealt with privately.

Ensure you have a simple process in place for routing these issues. An effective approach is to show empathy and commitment to a resolution, before offering the supporter the email address or phone number of a member of the club [not a company contact e.g. info@acme.com] who can help them resolve the matter.

Sometimes, of course, a response is not necessary or appropriate. There may be certain complaint types that cannot be satisfactorily addressed in social media and are better left alone. Or there may be certain types of user your club doesn't want to engage with, such as those or who share inappropriate content. Think about the instances in which your club would choose not to respond.

Recording new FAQs [for your FAQs]

It's highly likely that you'll get asked the same questions repeatedly, especially when launching kits, season tickets etc. It's always preferable to fully resolve a query in full view of the public and receive the benefit of that positive conclusion.

However, in-depth advice is more effectively given on a dedicated FAQs page or blog post on your website. This is particularly relevant for multi-step how-to content and multimedia. The ultimate aim is to be as useful to your supporters and partners as possible. This helps customer service efforts on social media by providing satisfactory endpoints for supporters.

Staffing social media for customer service

Through this section, you will be shown the basics of great customer service on social media and how to engage with your fans and audience.

What underpins great customer service on social media?

The key to strong customer service in social media is an organised team [even if you are a team of one, you will still need this process] with streamlined processes.

If you are not set up to promptly resolve issues and answer queries, this will put your club at risk. When people have a bad experience, not only do they cease to become a customer [in terms of quantity of purchases from the club], but they WILL tell others.

On the other hand, positive engagements with supporters can create a deep and loyal relationship.

Proactive and Reactive

It is important to implement two distinct streams of customer service:

- **Proactive customer care**: Look for ways where you can add value or solve a problem, BEFORE a supporter asks you to do it.
- **Reactive customer service**: Happens in response to a customer contacting your club.

Whilst the reactive service you provide is a basic requirement in today's social landscape, some of the smarter clubs online are going one step further and seeking out opportunities to provide help, even when there has been no explicit query directed at the club.

Tone of voice in customer service

Your club should have a defined tone of voice across social media content. While your tone should stay relatively defined, it may need to be adapted now and again for certain customer service interactions.

Think about how you can take your existing social media tone-of-voice and bring the following qualities into it:

Conciliatory
Show empathy and care for your supporters. They need to feel like there is a real person behind the response, someone who cares about their issue.

Serious
While your content may be designed to entertain followers when an issue occurs, a customer needs to know you are taking it seriously. Avoid trivialising issues through an excessively light or flippant tone in your responses.

Action-focused
Your customer service responses must be focused on what is going to happen and when. This is rarely necessary for other content pieces. However, when issues arise customers need to know that action is being taken, what the solution will look like, and when that is likely to happen.

Rules of engagement

With your social customer service team in place [or yourself as a one-person team], there must be a clear process for engaging with queries.

These rules of engagement are likely to cover the following areas:

Notifications

Employ the various notification mechanisms of each social platform accordingly. Today, these can be set up to trigger mobile notifications, emails or SMS messages.

Ensure that an agreed group of people are notified immediately when there is a query. If possible, include staff or volunteers who have different working full or part time working schedules to cover as much of the day as possible.

Most notifications will be non-urgent [dependent on club size], but there will be some that potentially present a club emergency. Take time to plot out all possible categories of issues and agree on a level of urgency with response times for each.

It is vital that you have this plan in place before you are hit by an emergency.

Query routing

Be clear on who can answer and who can resolve each potential query. Document and share it with all frontline social media staff so they are clear how to get issues resolved as quickly as possible.

Routing Queries Example

Here is an example of how your query routing can be set up.

30 minutes – major issues
- Escalate immediately to person responsible for PR, Marketing or Communications [email & phone]
- Inform social media manager immediately [email & phone]
- Responsible person and Social Media Manager will handle response within 30 minutes

1 hour – medium issues
- Show empathy & request their name, phone number and email address within 1 hour
- Inform Social Media Manager immediately [email & phone]

2 hours – minor issues
- Show empathy & request their name, phone number and email address or direct then to the relevant information within 2 hours

Taking issues offline

There may be a clear point at which it is preferable to take customer service conversations off public forums to resolve privately.

If you require name, contact details or addresses, you must take this offline and out of the public eye.

If a supporter or customer offers this information, you should ask them to delete ASAP.

For your club, deciding whether to take issues offline may be less clear. Imagine how your most likely queries might play out and decide some basic rules for taking them offline.

Standardised responding

Over time you'll notice that your responses will start to become repetitive. Many customer service and social media management platforms provide 'canned response' functionality, and this can be manually facilitated. A simple shared spreadsheet of the most common responses to regular queries is sufficient for many teams and can be shared and updated as time goes on. Again, if you keep this on Google Docs, all members of the team [if more than just one] will have access.

Ensure that when you use these canned responses, you personalise customer details, and refer to their unique situation. Appearing to publish robotic, pre-prepared, responses can be damaging to your club.

Closing issues and learnings

Remember that every public customer service query is an opportunity for your club to show the world who you are, what your values are, and what you think of your supporters.

Whether or not a query is taken offline, you must ensure that you have closed the loop on every single one. If, for example, you take an issue offline, remember to come back to the public conversation and thank the supporter for their query before asking if there's anything else you can do for them. This shows the world that you put your supporter first and can resolve issues as they arise.

Additionally, find the time on a regular basis [every week or month depending on volume] to conduct a review of recent customer service requests and how they were handled. Look at those which went well, as well as the ones that could have gone better, asking why they failed and set out how this type of interaction should be handled in the future.

PR disasters, recovery & contingency

In this section, we'll use a selection of real-world examples to show you how you should respond to a PR disaster, and what preventive measures you can take to reduce the risk.

What is a PR disaster in social media?

A disaster on social media can manifest itself in two ways - a misstep by a club's social media profile that creates negative PR across all channels, or a wider club issue which generates negative media, triggering dissent on social media platforms.

Either way, from a social media perspective, the effect will be the same; negative messages and mentions on a much larger scale than you would normally deal with. This will undoubtedly put stress on your processes and people. It is important you make sure the club is as prepared as possible to face this eventuality.

How do we scale up in these unpredictable circumstances?

Predictably, the answer is preparation, preparation, preparation. Thinking of a response only after a situation happens is not an effective strategy. By the time it happens, it will be too late to find a solution. Good recoveries are planned, agreed and documented to be ready for when a response is needed.

The best form of preparation is building a loyal, forgiving, audience through your day-to-day content publishing. How you publish in 'peacetime' tees up how you will publish when things go wrong.

Having an authentic, trust-based relationship with your fans and audience in which you truthfully reflect who you are as a club, and what your values are, will make talking about negative events easier, if and when they happen.

If you have already set the foundations for a trusted relationship with your supporters, using your everyday tone and trust in a disaster recovery situation can even develop and deepen the relationship with your social media followers.

How to respond

While your club will have a unique set of challenges and needs in this type of situation, there are some general rules to follow when responding to a crisis on social media.

The following will help mitigate the negative impact these situations can cause:

Apologise

First and foremost, never be above saying sorry. Do it quickly and sincerely. Clubs who apologise late will attract even more negative PR. Clubs who publish cold, insincere apologies that lack authenticity will almost certainly draw further dissent.

Publish your apology in the mediums that your audience is most comfortable with and that allows you to communicate on the most human level.

This example from Adidas, which was published in the wake of an insensitive marketing email subject line ['Congrats, you survived the Boston Marathon!'] shows restraint and grave seriousness around a tragedy which they showed a perceived insensitivity towards.

It might have seemed safer for the brand to ignore the issue, in fear of bringing more attention to it. But, they made this decision that it was more important to apologise and use this as an opportunity to show the brand wasn't afraid to put its hands up and accept that an error had been made. As you can see, the responses were mostly positive and understanding.

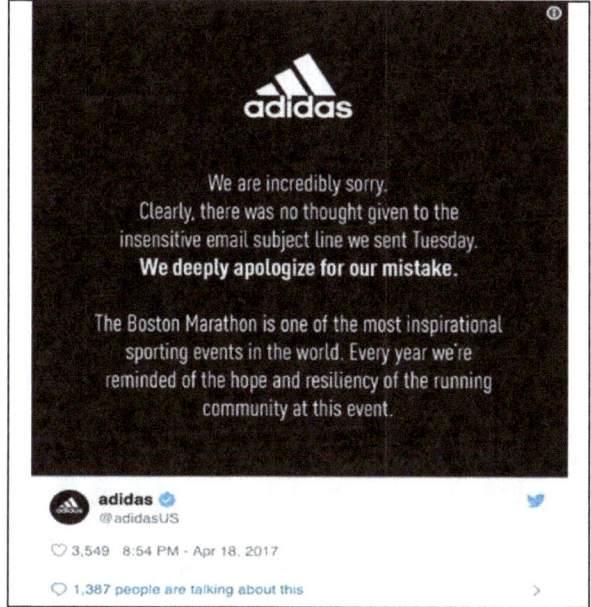

We are incredibly sorry.
Clearly, there was no thought given to the
insensitive email subject line we sent Tuesday.
We deeply apologize for our mistake.

The Boston Marathon is one of the most inspirational
sporting events in the world. Every year we're
reminded of the hope and resiliency of the running
community at this event.

adidas ✓
@adidasUS

♡ 3,549   8:54 PM · Apr 18, 2017

💬 1,387 people are talking about this

Empathise

In social media customer service, empathy is key. When issues arise, people need to know that your club is made of real people, and it is not faceless or uncaring.

Always start responses by telling customers what you know about how they're feeling e.g. "We know how frustrating and inconvenient the issue with the live stream was and...".

Be mindful of overused apology phrases. For instance, "we apologise for any inconvenience caused" is so widely used that it has lost much of its intended meaning and is becoming a hollow apology.

Make people feel heard

As well as demonstrating empathy with your supporters, it's crucial that they feel heard when things go wrong. From their perspective, they've chosen to spend time and/ or money with your club and that's an investment they could have placed elsewhere.

You must give supporters a chance to say what they think and feel, even when you know it's not going to be good. Just be prepared to hear those concerns and respond to them appropriately.

Being right, or winning the debate, doesn't matter

In today's social media landscape, many of us are fuelled by the need to be proven right and prove others wrong. It's the fuel that keeps a million arguments raging across the internet every minute of every day. While individuals can do this, as a professional organisation you cannot follow this trend.

The more authenticity, candour and human sincerity you can put into your responses to online negativity, the further you will go to promote a more balanced view of your club in the midst of a storm.

As a representative of a club, you can only go so far in explaining why things have happened and what you are doing to solve the issues. You should make authentic gestures and show how you're changing to mitigate for the future, but you can't win everyone over and you never will. Stay above arguments and debates, state your case in the most truthful, helpful, way possible.

Stay clear and results-focused

As mentioned in the previous section, it's crucial that your responses remain focused on resolution while also showing that you care and understand your supporters' needs. This should be reinforced by taking demonstrable steps towards a clear and observable resolution.

Strip away ambiguity and show that steps are being taken to help your supporter. People understand that you are not perfect, but they will only continue to spend money with you if they know that you're continually striving to improve your offering for them and your wider impact on the world.

Take preventative measures

Some issues cannot be foreseen or prevented from happening again, but the majority can. After a PR disaster, always consider how changes could be made to prevent the same mistake from being made again.

In the case of Adidas, sending out a test email to an internal seed list two hours before broadcast could eliminate any last-minute PR disasters. While audiences can easily forgive a mistake the first time, they are likely to perceive it as a lack of care the second time.

It is important to learn from other companies' social media disasters.

Remember:

1. **Apologise**
2. **Empathise**
3. **Make your audience feel heard Don't try to be 'right'**
4. **Focus on resolution**

Insights & Analysis

To determine whether the work you are doing is valuable for your club, you must first set your SMART objectives.

This will help you understand how your activity can support your club goals. By using SMART objectives, it is simple to measure and report on what you have, and have not, achieved. Measuring and reporting on your objectives is your "analysis".

In addition to analysis, you should also look for insights to understand how to further improve your performance. You should gather insights from a host of different sources across your club. They help you develop a deeper understanding of your supporters, their preferences, and the external environments which influence them.

These insights will give you the grounding you need to create a relevant and effective strategy.

Platform insights

Not only does social media provide a platform for marketers to communicate with their audiences but it also allows you to learn about our audience. For a football club, this lets you find out more about your supporters than has ever been possible.

We gain insights into their personalities, interests, social habits, behaviours, and content consumption patterns.

The information we acquire through social media should inform our future marketing decisions and improve our overall output. It should also stop you from repeating past mistakes and, in time, increase the quality [value and relevance to the supporters] of your content.

There are multiple sources from which you can gain data. There's also a selection of marketing platforms which will aggregate this data for you. However, these can be expensive and learning how to do this process manually will give you an invaluable understanding of each data source.

Facebook

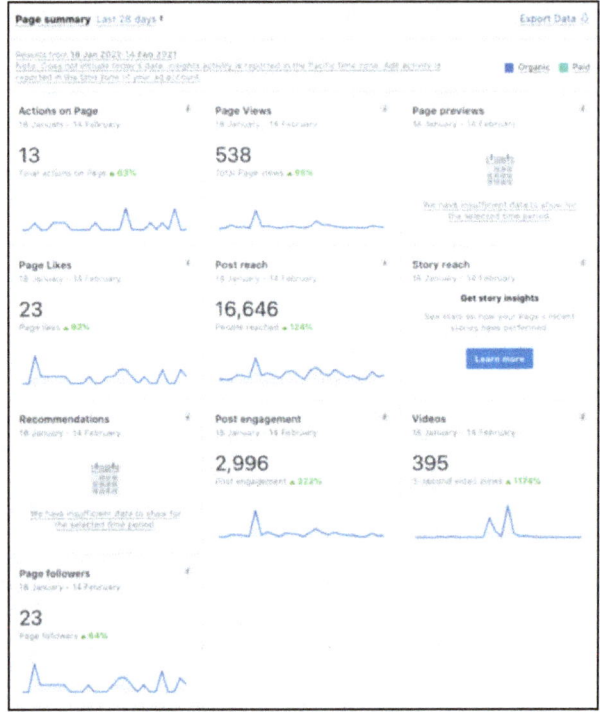

Facebook offers an Insights platform to those who have a business page, providing a variety of information about your audience and the content you publish there.

If your club is registered as a person and not a business, make sure you change over to a business account immediately. It's free and opens up all the insights and analysis you need to promote your club and learn about your audience.

The metrics that you can track include:

Actions on page
The number of clicks on your page's contact info and call-to-action button.

Page views
The number of times a page's profile has been viewed by logged-in and logged-out people.

Page previews
The number of times people hovered over your page name or profile picture to see a preview of your page's content.

Page likes
The number of new people who have liked your page broken down by paid and non-paid.

Post reach
The number of people who had any posts from your page on their screen, broken down by total, organic, and promotions.

Recommendations
The number of times people recommended your page to friends on Facebook.

Post engagements
The number of times people have engaged with your posts through likes, comments, shares and more.

Responsiveness
Your response rate is the percentage of messages you responded to in messenger. Response time is the average time it took for your page to respond to a message, based on the fastest 90% of response times in Messenger.

Videos
The number of times your page's videos played for at least 3 seconds, or for nearly their total length if they're shorter than 3 seconds, broken down by total, paid, and non-paid.

Page followers
The number of new people who have followed your Facebook page broken down by paid and non-paid.

X [Twitter]

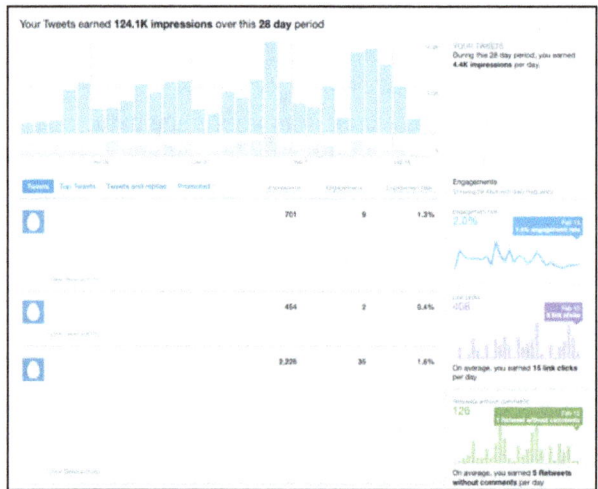

Whilst X Analytics is somewhat simpler than Facebook, their in-platform insights is a necessary and valuable tool in determining the success of your content.

Posts
This is the number of times you have posted in any defined date range.

Post impressions
The number of times people saw a post.

Post engagements
How many times someone interacted in any way with your post. This includes clicks on your images, links, profile and hashtags. It also includes expands, likes, reposts, replies and follows.

Profile visits
The number of visits to your X profile [X.com/yourusername] from all internal and external sources.

Mentions
The number of times your handle [@yourusername] has been included in the text of another user's post.

Followers
This is the total number of followers you have, with the change over the previous period. You can also see how many followers you gained or lost each month in the overview dashboard.

In addition, X has an Audience dashboard which offers a number of insights into your audience and other segments of X's wider audience. Through partnerships with data companies, X has matched user records to provide information such as; demographics, consumer behaviour, lifestyle, interests, jobs, and technology footprint.

These differences should guide you on how to cater to your audience and be of most value to them, but also on how to attract other specific audience-types, based on what they will respond strongly to.

X is constantly changing and becoming almost unstable. By the time you read this book, many of the items above may not be available, or have been changed or moved.

Instagram

The mobile-first image and video platform has a stripped-down insight product, allowing owners of pages that have registered as businesses to view key summary data about their posts and audience.

Similar to Facebook, it is free to register your club as a business on Instagram and you should do that at the earliest opportunity.

You can access top-line stats about your feed posts, stories and ads ['promotions'] in the form of the following:

- o **Impressions** - views of the content
- o **Engagement** - likes, comments or clicks on posts
- o **Unique views** - people who have seen the content
- o **Profile visits** - visits to your profile page

In addition, there is data about your audience on Instagram, such as:

Discovery
How many accounts you reached in total per day over the last week.

Followers
How many and the number lost or gained since the previous week.

Top locations
Where your followers are concentrated, by city or country.
Age range
How your audience is split between age groups.

Gender
The gender distribution of your followers.

Followers' active times
The days of the week, and hours of the day, that your followers are most active on Instagram. When looking at hours of the day

147

you can cycle through the days of the week to see hourly patterns on different days. These will likely be the same throughout the weekdays, and then different on the weekend.

Combining social with other data sources

As well as the platform analytics themselves, you can gain some useful insights from other tools within your marketing stack that will build a richer picture of your social media ROI.

Website analytics

Mapping your website analytics to social activity can generate valuable insights about your supporters. You can start to evaluate which channels and content drive the most value for your club. This data will also tell you how different supporters respond to your social output and how they then behave when navigating your website.

In Google Analytics, much of this evaluation will rely on the setting up of goals i.e. certain pages or actions on the site that represent a financial value to the club, such as the sale of replica kits. In such instances, this sale would end in completion or 'Thank You' page, visiting which would trigger a goal in analytics.

You can set up goals in the admin page on Google analytics.

Based on the existence of such goals, you can start to combine dimensions in your reports in the following ways to gain insights:

Source / Goal Value

This tells you the average value of users from different sources. For instance, are Twitter/X users creating more revenue than Facebook users? And how much does it cost to acquire each one?

Content / Goal Value

These dimensions will show what commercial value specific pieces of social media content present to the business.

Source / Goal Conversion Rate

Shows the true propensity of visitors from different social platforms to perform valuable actions on your site. You may, for instance, find that whilst Facebook visitors are more frequent, Instagram visitors are more likely to convert.

In addition to gaining insight into your social media audience visiting your website, you can use data on how people find and navigate your site to inform social content strategy.

Depending on your website, you may have some, all of none of the following approaches available. If you're unsure or need direct instructions on how to use or find them, please contact your web developer.

Approach 1

By looking at the most viewed pages on your site you can start to determine which aspects of your club's offering people are most interested in.

Approach 2

If you have a search function on your site, you can see what searches visitors are making and identify some informational needs of your supporters to better serve through social content.

Approach 3

Where do people tend to wander off your site? Identifying these fewer compelling aspects of your communications could help to improve social media output.

Approach 4

Gained through Google Search Console, insight into which queries you rank for, and which ones generate traffic can be an invaluable source of the informational needs you could meet in social.

Knowing which other websites, blogs and articles are linking to you will offer a better understanding of your supporters and their online consumption habits so that you can cater to them more relevantly in social.

Email marketing platform

If you're lucky enough to deliver email communications, the results from these efforts should be shared with your social content team - and vice versa [if the teams are different].

In many cases email is a more direct channel for clubs, offering unfiltered access to people who have engaged or shown interest previously. There is little intervention from algorithms or competition with advertising allowing email content to be seen by many, and not just by the most engaged users [as with social]. So given this scale, data points can be statistically relevant, even for small clubs.

You can use a free Email Service Provider, such as Mail Chimp [www.mailchimp.com] to build and send emails and will also include some insights and analysis on your email campaign data.

Ensure that you take this data and analyse what email subject lines work [generate highest open rates], and how you could work elements of the most successful ones into your social media copy. Investigate which stories or products recipients click on - and which ones they don't - to add an additional layer of understanding about the content that resonates with your most engaged fans.

Customer service

Your interactions with supporters in a customer service manner can reveal insights into further informational needs of your supporters.

Perform regular [at least monthly] reviews of queries to discover the most frequent questions. While these can feed into an FAQ page on your website, you can reach more of your supporters and customers by proactively creating content about these things.

Feed these proactive pieces into your Help content each month. These will, primarily, be published as organic social media posts, not supported with ad budget, as they are targeted at your existing audience.

When measuring their ROI take into account that their purpose is not necessarily to drive mass reach or high engagement. It is to better inform your supporters and put your commitment to customer care on public display.

Surveys

Large clubs regularly survey supporters, you should also try to tap into this invaluable information. It will give you insight into how your club, and its various departments, are perceived by the outside world. This can help inform your approach to messaging, content opportunities and aid benchmarking against the type of comments you receive through social channels.

If you plan to conduct a survey, make sure that you are equipped and empowered to deal with any potential responses. If a fan complains about a toilet that you just can't fix, it's going to look worse in the long-term if that same issue arises repeatedly.

Recording your social media metrics and turning them into insights

Through this section, you will become familiar with tools and techniques to record your social media metrics and monitor your social media performance.

Creating a supporter-first social media strategy

A supporter-first strategy means that you are putting your supporters at the centre of everything that your club does. With this strategy, any decision that you make should be measured against how effective it is to your supporter experience.

Developing an effective supporter-first social media strategy is achieved by:

1. Pull your data together to create a picture of your supporters.
2. Make observations about the picture.
3. Draw hypotheses or conclusions based on your observations.
4. Set actions to help prove or disprove any hypotheses – your test plan.

This method of developing your test plan is built upon testing variables to give your audiences what they want and help achieve your objective.

Throughout this section, you will be guided through a reporting template. You should use the template to record your social media results and identify common trends in your best, and worst, performing posts. You can find the template at this link http://bit.ly/3bbKGLl.

This template will help you to create truly actionable insights - as opposed to mere measurements. It's important to communicate the highlights of your findings to those who don't work with social media on a daily basis.

Remember that some colleagues may not have a thorough understanding of how social media marketing works or the significance of certain metrics.

You will discover a process for gathering your metrics and presenting them in a way which is simple to analyse. Finally, you will learn how to create the type of insights that will inform your next steps and improve your decision making.

Performance against objectives

Objectives	KPI target <month>	KPI Actual <month>	% difference
Objective 1			
Objective 2			
Objective 3			

Objectives	KPI target - year to date	KPI Actual - year to date	% difference
Objective 1			
Objective 2			
Objective 3			

Include campaign or channel objectives here. Insert: how you are performing for that month in the top table, and what you are achieving so far for the year in the bottom.

The first and most important thing is to monitor your progress towards your objectives. This will set the tone for the rest of the report.

Do you need big changes to your approach to reach your objectives? Or are you on track but need to monitor and tweak to ensure you stay on the right path?

There are two key ways to measure your targets: individual months, and accrued measure.

The accrued measure or 'year to date' [YTD] will tell you your overall performance. Be aware that there are always peaks and troughs in performance. Being below your objective for one month isn't a problem if you've exceeded in previous months. Or, if you excel in one month, you may be taking the opportunity to make up for where you have fallen short in previous months.

You will see the top table focuses on your performance for the month you are reporting on, and the second table focuses on your YTD performance.

Follower Trends

To help create an at-a-glance view of the number of followers you have this month, last month and this month last year, you can present the follower trends as a graph.

It also allows you to discover and document seasonal trends and steady growth [or decline] in a simple way.

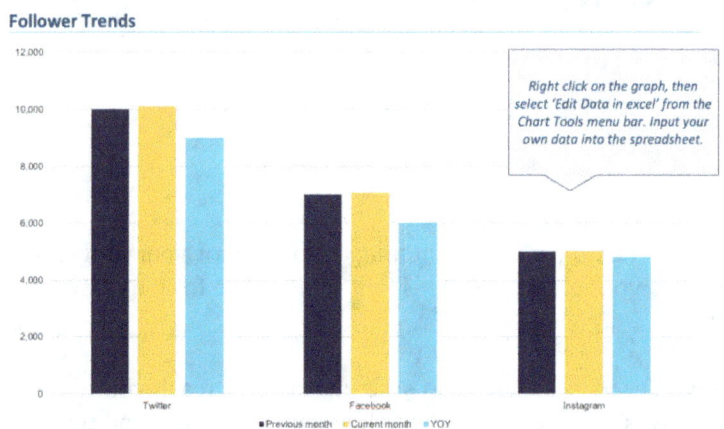

Right click on the graph, then select 'Edit Data in excel' from the menu bar. Input your own data into the spreadsheet. [Although this document is a PowerPoint presentation, you will still be able to edit the data in excel, so long as you have access to these Microsoft programs].

If your follower numbers are declining, you need to work out the trigger. Below are a number of common causes and how you could respond to them.

- o Your audience is becoming bored with what you are posting: Look for poor performing content and explore how you can give it a refresh.

- o A change somewhere that your audience doesn't approve of: This is why closely monitored testing of one variable

155

at a time is advisable. If your current test isn't working, drop it and move on.

o A conscious strategic decision to focus on a niche more engaged audience: Hoorah! It may be working, check your engagement rates to confirm either way. If your engagement isn't up – try something new to entertain your niche target audience.

o The reputation of your club is damaging your performance: Have you had a PR disaster in the last month? If so, start building a content strategy to rebuild trust. Be transparent about the problem, add some humour if appropriate, and be clear about how you are fixing it.

o Or, it could be something completely outside of your control. For example, you may have attracted a high number of automated bot followers, and the platform is removing them. Or users are moving away from a now unfashionable social network.

Content and reach interactions

Are you providing content that your audience can relate to, or sees as something they want to share? Is the engagement rate at a high enough level to indicate to social platforms that they should add your content to organic feeds and algorithms?

Current Reach

Platform	This month	YOY / Objective [delete as appropriate]	% difference
Social Media			
Facebook			
Instagram			
Twitter			

Add up the reach for each platform that you use and input it into the table. If you have an objective for reach, use this in the '3rd column. Alternatively, benchmark against the same month in the previous year (YOY). This will be a good indicator of progress. You can add rows if needed

Calculate the reach for each platform that you use and add it into the table. If you have an objective for reach [eg. Generate a monthly social media reach of 1,000,000 users in FY24], use this in the 3rd column. Alternatively, you can set a benchmark against the same month in the previous year. This year-on-year measure [YOY] is a good indicator of progress.

Total Interactions

Platform	This month	YOY / Objective [delete as appropriate]	% difference
Social Media			
Facebook			
Instagram			
Twitter			

Add up the total interactions for each platform that you use and input it into the table. If you have an objective for interactions, use this in the 3rd column. Alternatively, benchmark against the same month in the previous year (YOY). This will be a good indicator of progress. You can add rows if needed

Calculate the total interactions for each platform that you use and input it into the table. If you have an objective for interactions use this in the '3rd column. Again, you can benchmark against the same month in the previous year.

You will hopefully see upward trends here. If there are downward trends, have a look at how you can change your content to improve the performance.

Assessing the effectiveness of your content
Determining the success of your content would be an unmanageable task if you tried to analyse and draw insights from every single post.

To keep the amount of analysis time to a reasonable level, focus on...
- the top-performing content
- the worst or underperforming content.

Step 1: Top-performing content

Gather screenshots of the top and bottom performers across each platform. If you have posted content to perform a specific test [such as post time, post length, hashtags use etc.] then you should also take a note of it here.

Adapt the template, adding in extra slides, depending on how you want to categorise your content performance.

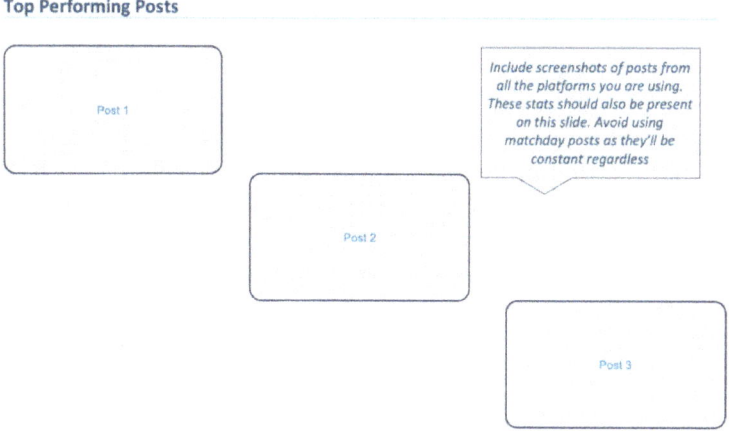

158

Include screenshots of posts from all the platforms you are using. The stats should also be present on this slide.

Step2: Observation

Look through all of the posts you have collected and see what jumps out at you, you should then record all of your observations about these posts.

Do your observations confirm your current practices? Are your top performers the content you expected?

Engagement trends

Your engagement trends are just as important as the performance of individual posts.

It doesn't matter how great your posts are if you put them out at the wrong times. Or, if you don't understand your overarching content trends. For example, an offer for Mothers' Day hospitality will probably attract more positive interactions in March than in November.

By putting your posts out at optimum times, you will immediately gain interactions, increasing the popularity and in turn the 'ranking' of your post by the platform algorithms.

When you understand the overarching content variable trends, you will resist the temptation to make knee-jerk decisions based on individual anomalies.

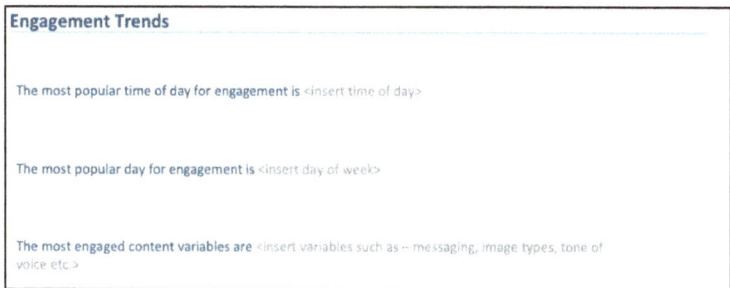

Test results

You will use your test results, as well as the trends you have seen, to inform what you do going forward.

This is a highlight report, so you don't need to include outcomes from every test you run. Focus on those tests that will inform a change in practices or demonstrate that you should continue as you are with a specific variable.

Inconclusive tests, for example, don't need to be included.

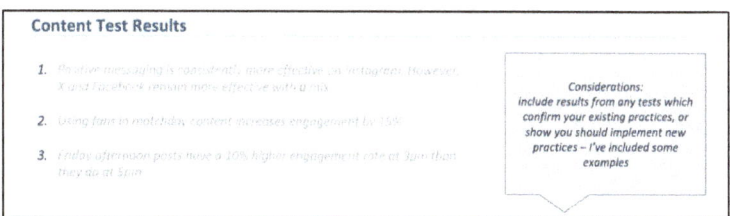

Hypotheses

All of your observations, trends and test results will form a picture of what your supporters do or don't want from you.

At this point, you have a choice, take what you believe to be true from these and implement them all immediately. If you have a small team, or you are the only one who works on your social channels, this could be the most efficient path for you. However, you won't be able to track exactly which change has been the contributing factor.

Alternatively, you can treat them as a hypothesis to test, before implementing them. This way you will address each variable at a time, stress testing how reliable the change in performance is.

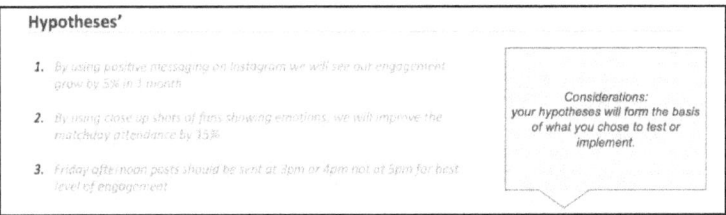

The hypotheses' that you create, will inform your ongoing test plan.

Actions

The final stage in this reporting and analysis process is to decide what actions you will take. This stage is a combination of implementing new practices and putting variables to the test.

The aim is for these actions to further improve the value and enjoyment of your content to your audience and, therefore, improve your performance.

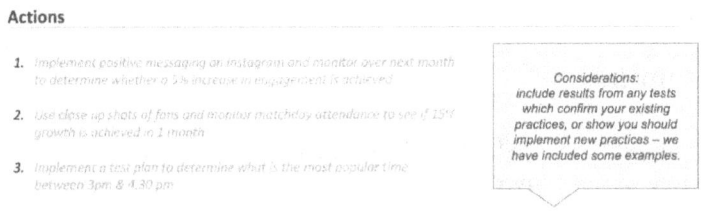

Within the template, you will find some examples of what these actions may look like.

Always improve your social media performance

By the end of this section, you will feel confident making iterative improvements using your test and learn programme.

Understanding your social media metrics

Many marketers simply run through the creation process, seeing their ideas through to production and publication without a plan for how they will optimise their content through data and learnings over time.

Social media provides us with an opportunity to test new ideas, segment our audiences, and tweak our creative approach to provide the best possible content.

What are the different ways to measure Social Media performance?

Social media metrics usually stem from a few different categories which cover key objectives such as…
- Engagement
- Conversion
- Sentiment
- Exposure

Engagement

How deep is the relationship between your club and its followers/ customers? Engagement is important in building reach and loyalty.

- o Is there a correlation between engagement and content type?
- o Are there certain photos or creative assets that do better than others?
- o How many times has someone marked a specific post as spam?

- o What types of engagements are the most popular [usually it will be those which require the least commitment e.g. a like or a retweet].
- o What was going on in the user's world at the time a post was made? Think about news headlines, seasonal events, or life stage milestones.

Conversion

Vital for sales or to encourage sharing. Driving action is important in all marketing but is sometimes forgotten in social media.

- o If there was a call-to-action on a post, did users respond in the desired manner?
  - o Did they click the link to view your content?
  - o Did they answer the question?
  - o Did they sign up for your newsletter?
  - o Did they buy a shirt?
- o If not, what did they do instead [if anything]?
- o How are social platforms driving traffic to your club's website?
- o What is the conversion rate from social commerce buttons?

Sentiment

How do people feel about your club? Typically, sentiment is measured as positive, negative or neutral.

- o What is the nature of the comments that your social media posts receive?
- o What is the nature of the messages and feedback communities provide unrelated to content? Testimonials or praise? Complaints? Neutral items [like questions]?
- o What is the nature of the conversation about the brand [this needs you to actively listen to your fans on social media]?

Exposure

It is important to understand reach in context. A high level of exposure may not be as important as reaching a small number of specific individuals.

- o How many people saw your content compared to the number of people in your fan base?
- o What's the average reach, per platform?
- o Is there a trend [e.g. time of day, or day of the week etc.] where things are higher or lower than the average?

A framework for test and learn tactics

The first thing you'll need to be clear about is your club goals, and how your social media objectives contribute to them. Once you're clear on your most important social KPI, you can use it as a benchmark for your test evaluations.

For example, if your goal is club awareness, and the social metric supporting it is reach, you will then look at the success of each piece of content in terms of the number of people reached and the number of impressions.

Then, you will decide which variables you can test over time.

These should include:

- o **Platform** - which platform you publish on
- o **Day** - which day of the week
- o **Time** - which hour of the day
- o **Format** - what form your content takes, for example: image, multi-image, carousel, video, audio, or text-only

You should also consider more granular details, such as:

Imagery type

Testing different approaches to imagery in your still and moving visuals. Try testing opposing techniques against each other to build up an idea of what works. Examples include; photographic vs illustrated, product vs lifestyle shot, players vs models, and casual vs formal.

Emotional copy angle

Different people respond to different emotional hooks. Try testing a number of different styles including:
- Fear of loss/ fear of missing out [FOMO]
- Positive
- Negative
- Straightforward
- Amusing
- Motivational

Content length

Test short vs long videos and text content

Set a monthly review cycle

Every month, when you set out the upcoming month's content calendar, take some time to review the previous month and record your test results in the accompanying template.

Include those variables which have previously worked well into your next months' content. Continue to test them against new variables to find your sweet spots.

Share these results across your team via regular monthly reports. These should discuss what you tested and what worked. Don't be afraid to embrace some element of failure. The digital landscape you operate in requires that we fail regularly. Every time you execute marketing in today's world you are inevitably taking a risk because the results are always unpredictable to some extent.

It can feel unnatural to be open about this potential failure to those you report to, your colleagues, clients, as well as those who report to you. You just need to focus on your set test-and-learn framework. Failures are a key part of the process through which you are finding the types and styles of content that the key segments of your supporters respond strongly to.

Is it possible to calculate social media ROI?

ROI is one of the few genuine financial measures of marketing success and is directly comparable to metrics used by financial investors in respect of business more generally. When you're using your social media content to drive sales, calculating an ROI on your activity can prove a useful activity.

Where ROI can be attributed specifically to one or more promotional activities it is a very powerful metric. Unfortunately, the question remains: how can we attribute the outcome of certain activities to the social media activity that preceded it?

Social media ROI is the financial return from all the time, effort, and resources committed to social media marketing, and it is best calculated with numerical/monetary amounts. Unfortunately, there are no pound signs directly attributable to retweets or likes.

Facebook and Twitter/X, for example, are potentially an almost zero- pound investment as there is no cost from these networks to create a brand page. However, there can be other costs for content creation and resources to manage campaigns. Additional costs will incur if you use paid for social media advertising.

In theory, therefore, social media is low cost [providing that you don't pay too much for ads] and should produce strong returns as a result.

In order to track ROI:

- o Identify the monetary investment in social media
- o Attach a pounds and pence amount to the social media goals

Calculating the return on investment [ROI]

Calculating return is one of the more difficult elements of social media ROI because it can mean so many different things to so many different marketers. For example, it was historically very common to tie social media return to direct sales.

While social commerce is possible in some platforms, for many social media campaigns the objectives are around engagement, reach and reputation which are measured by other criteria than sales.

When calculating ROI:

- o Choose the goal – this can be anything from new followers to spending time on a certain webpage
- o Track the goal - choose the goal and begin to track it using all the tools at your disposal
- o Assign a monetary value - is it Lifetime Value [LTV], average sales, etc.

How do we calculate social media ROI?

While it is true that participation on X, Facebook, and other platforms is free, time is not. Social media tools may not be free, and ad spend has a direct cost.

Social media ROI is your financial return from all the resources, time and energy spent on social media.

When calculating ROI you must have a full understanding of 'I' which is your investment.

Three simple elements you need to add up to calculate your investment are listed below:
- o **Your time** - multiply your labour cost per hour by the number of hours committed over a given period. This may be £0 if working with volunteers. [Depending on

whether you're measuring social media ROI for the week, the month, per campaign, etc.].

- o **Your social media tools** – add up the costs of all the tools and services you use for social media. Find the weekly or monthly costs [divide annual fees by 52 for the weekly cost, and by 12 for the monthly cost].
- o **Your advertising spend** – calculate the amount you spend on social media advertising boosting Facebook posts, promoting tweets, etc.

You will also need to measure the value of your social media activity. This will most likely be through Season Ticket sales, kit launches etc. Although very hard to get an exact amount, you can use previous season's figures to determine your impact through social media.

To calculate ROI:

Social media ROI % = [[Value generated from social media – Costs of social media investment] / Costs of social media investment] * 100

EXERCISE

- If you generate £5,000 in kit sales from a £500 social media ad spend, what is your social media ROI?

Is there an alternative to measuring ROI?

Although ROI is a very good measure for social media activity because it allows a ready comparison for all other types of media, it can sometimes be difficult to use if there are no sales or tracking.

A good alternative is the **Social Equivalent Advertising Value [SEAV].**

This is where you calculate how much you would have needed to spend to generate the result if you were paying for advertising such as display. Put simply, it is the value of the social activity measured in the savings from advertising.

For example:

If 200 clicks to your website would cost £10/click in display advertising and you managed to get 200 clicks from your social media activity for free.

The **SEAV** = number of website clicks x cost per click from traditional advertising = an SEAV of £2,000.

Final Thoughts

If you don't have any marketing spend then it will always be difficult to calculate a financial ROI. However, you should always be mindful of the time and effort that you're spending on your content and always ask yourself if the effort is worth the reward. Sometimes it won't be, and that's fine. Don't burn yourself out trying to deliver hundreds of pieces of content if the output isn't justified.

Final Thoughts & Live Examples

This section wraps up everything that's been covered and shows how to use it with live examples from my time at Stenhousemuir FC.

Planning Laydowns

Content planning is extremely important for any football club. By delivering consistent comms, you can ensure that your fans are always kept up to date with the relevant information. If your planning is correct, you will deliver the right information at the right time ensuring maximum engagement.

Whereas important information is held on the content planner, a useful weekly laydown approach can be essential to ensure that you deliver the required content. At Stenhousemuir, we have a weekly version and a matchday version, making sure that nothing is missed, and we deliver consistent and engaging comms to our fans. You can find templates for the weekly content laydown and the matchday content laydown here https://bit.ly/FootballMarketing

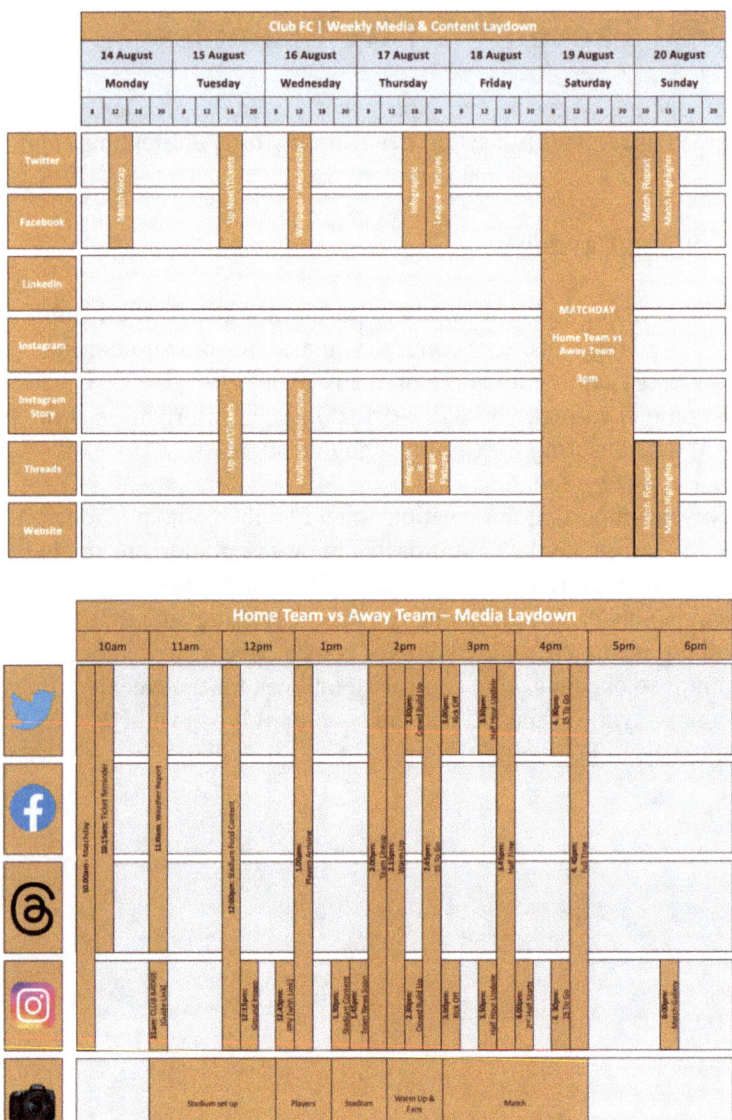

Media Shoots

If you're at a part-time club, getting the players for a media photo shoot may prove tricky.

The most important things to do when planning a photoshoot;

- Calculate how much time you will have with the players
- Make a list of each piece of content you want to capture from each player
- Prioritise your images to ensure that you get the most important pieces
- Create a plan to share with the players beforehand to ensure you use their time efficiently

STENHOUSEMUIR FC MEDIA SHOOT
Tuesday 8 August 5.30pm

Straight ahead [arms behind back]

Straight ahead [arms folded]

Straight ahead [looking at badge]

Facing right [with ball] + facing left [with ball]

Straight ahead [with ball]

Facing right [arms behind back] + facing left [arms behind back]

Straight ahead [left arm point] + Straight ahead [right arm point]

Player goal celebration [image only]

Note to players:
Please wear football boots as full length pictures will be taken
We'll be photographing away kits first, and then home kits
Feel free to bring props for your goal celebration pose
Photographer will be set up in viewing gallery
Backroom staff photos will also be taken [face and side on only]
Once all players have been done, there will be a squad picture on the pitch

For this photoshoot, we scheduled 20 minutes per player [for home and away kits]. If you don't have so much time for each player, make sure you prioritise your requirements. It is better to get just one picture each of 20 players, than 20 different pictures of only one player.

Stenhousemuir FC examples

Finally, I've included how some of the pieces included in this book translate to an actual football club's social media accounts.

Profile and Cover Photos

Make sure that your club is identifiable through your cover photo across all social media channels. Always make sure that your profile photo is an uncropped image of your club's badge.

Reactive Content

Alongside your planned content, reactive content is a way for your club to put its unique spin on the events of the day [or even minute]. This can improve your reach and increase your audience.

Bring your fans on your journey

Your fans are the lifeblood of your club. Capture their emotion and bring them on your journey whenever you can.

Carousels

Carousel Ads allows you to drive people to a specific link through multiple images or videos — all within a single post.

You can build your X Carousels at https://ads.twitter.com

Instagram Stories

These are the stories that appear on the top banner in Instagram and should be 1080px x 1920px. There should primarily be matchday images as they'll disappear after 24 hours.

View a standard Stenhousemuir Matchday Instagram story at
https://bit.ly/SFC-IGStory

Key Information

A major part of your role in marketing your team is to give your fans all the information that they could need to have an easy matchday experience whether home or away.

For home matches, we have created a guide to Ochilview which highlights everything that a first-time fan would find useful. You can view this guide online here – https://bit.ly/OchilviewGuide

This was created on Adobe InDesign and uploaded to their publishing host.

For away matches, we pull out key information to help make the away trip as easy and as stress-free as possible. By pulling all the relevant information into your content, you can ensure that your fans have an easy matchday experience.

Next Steps

Whereas I do not expect that you will have to incorporate everything in this book into your social media and marketing strategy, I do hope there's enough in here to help make a difference in either your management of a football club's social media channels, or your journey to become involved at a football club.

For further support, you can join the Scottish Football Media Group on Discord. You can join the group here – https://bit.ly/FootballMedia

I can be personally contacted at ian.fitzpatrick82@gmail.com for further support or feedback.

Thank You

I need to say thank you to a few people that have helped me on my journey.

To Iain McMenemy and Jamie Sweeney, thank you for allowing me to do my thing at Stenhousemuir. Since day one, you were both fully supportive of my vision and were happy for me to take control and push Stenhousemuir's social media accounts and marketing onto the next level. Thanks also to Blair Cremin and David Alexander who have continued to support me at Ochilview.

Thanks to the media team at Stenhousemuir who helped me build my perfect team. Connor Ferguson, Rennie Hamilton, Angus Blacklock, Chris MacMillan, Raymond Davies and Aaron Marshall, thank you all for making my role one of the easiest in Scottish football. The effort and output that you all do is massively underrated, and you will all outgrow Stenhousemuir and move on to bigger things. It's a pleasure working with each one of you and I'm extremely proud of the work and content that we have produced at Stenhousemuir.

Thank you to my brother Steve who has guided, inspired and supported everything that I've ever done including helping with many reads, edits, re-reads and re-edits of this book!

Finally, thank you to the Scottish Football Media community for the inspiration and desire to take everything I do to the next level.

www.ingramcontent.com/pod-product-compliance
Lightning Source LLC
Chambersburg PA
CBHW072159290526
45794CB00004B/1573